78 Important Questions Every Leader Should Ask and Answer

78 Important Questions Every Leader Should Ask and Answer

CHRIS CLARKE-EPSTEIN

AMACOM AMERICAN MANAGEMENT ASSOCIATION
New York ▪ Atlanta ▪ Brussels ▪ Buenos Aires ▪ Chicago
London ▪ Mexico City ▪ San Francisco ▪ Shanghai ▪ Tokyo
Toronto ▪ Washington, D. C.

This publication is designed to provide accurate and authoritative information in regard to the subject matter covered. It is sold with the understanding that the publisher is not engaged in rendering legal, accounting, or other professional service. If legal advice or other expert assistance is required, the services of a competent professional person should be sought.

Library of Congress Cataloging-in-Publication Data

Clarke-Epstein, Chris.
   78 important questions every leader should ask and answer / Chris
   p. cm.
Includes bibliographical references (p.   ) and index.
   ISBN 0-8144-7162-5
   1. Leadership. 2. Communication in organizations. 3. Corporate culture.
4. Public relations. I. Title: Seventy eight important questions every leader
should ask and answer. II. Title.

HD57.7. C539 2002
658.4'092--dc21
                                                    2002008308

Printing number
10 9 8 7 6 5 4 3 2 1

To my mother, June Blomberg, who raised me in an environment that encouraged me to ask questions…lots of them.

To Stel Epstein and Miriam Phillips, who read everything I write and have the courage to ask, "What were you thinking?"

contents

preface

Captain Jean-Luc Picard looked up from his log, checked the chronometer and decided that he had spent enough time in his ready room for one day. Time to get up and walk about a bit, get the feel of the ship under his feet. A crew had moods and the only way to find out what they are is to go out and tread the deck. Of course, he could just call in either Riker or Troi and put the question to them—*How is the crew feeling?*—and from their different perspectives form a clear and reliable picture. Over the years, Picard had learned that this method omitted an essential component. If he stayed in his ready room and waited for subordinates to bring him answers, the crew wouldn't know how

Picard was feeling, at least, how Picard *wanted* them to
think he was feeling.

—Jeffrey Lang, *Immortal Coil*

When Tom Peters wrote *In Search of Excellence* in 1982, he introduced leaders all over the world to the concept of Managing by
Wandering Around (MBWA). As a consultant and facilitator for
management teams, I've discovered how difficult it is for many leaders to get up from behind their desks, or more frequently, to excuse
themselves from yet another meeting and place themselves in close
proximity to the people they are leading. One day it dawned on me
that getting them in front of their people isn't even the hardest part.
All too often, they don't know what to say once they get there!

You might have assumed that from the moment you were given
the title of leader, you were required to be the source of all wisdom.
In other words, you were supposed to be the person answering

**It is not the answer that en-
lightens, but the question.**

—Eugene Ionesco,
Romanian playwright

---

questions, not asking them. Nothing could be further from the
truth. Good leaders are humbled by the realization of all they do
not know, and they quickly reach the conclusion that they'd better
find some trusted advisers and ask a few questions. Great leaders
know that asking questions of a few won't give them enough data.
To succeed, they must make asking questions of anyone and everyone their top priority. Sometimes they must also answer difficult
questions—questions that they don't know the answer to or that

they can't answer without giving away confidential data or to which they know the answer will be unwelcome.

This behavior takes courage. Courage, because asking questions and admitting they don't know an answer are not behaviors people expect from leaders. Ask most people to describe a leader, and they'll use words such as "strong," "resourceful," "charismatic," "decisive," and "bold." If "curious," "inquisitive," and "questioning" get mentioned at all, they'll be at the end of the list. Mental models are hard to change, but this is one we must change. If leadership requires right answers all the time, then only few will qualify. If, however, leadership requires challenging questions, we can all aspire to the title of leader.

How to Use This Book

Approaching leadership with a questioning mindset may be easier than changing the embedded belief that a leader must be quick with an answer into the belief that a leader needs to be quick with a question.

If the concept of questions has caught your fancy, and if you believe that you need to try something new because your old leadership behaviors just don't seem to have the same impact, you and I are going to have some long hours and fun together. After you finish this section, you may want to go back to the Table of Contents and browse. There may be a question that catches your attention. It's okay—read that one first. I strongly suggest that you read the entire book (in any order) and think about the power of these questions before you start to ask them.

You must keep in mind that asking questions isn't the same as asking the right questions. If you aspire to be a leader in action as well as in title, you need to plan your questioning strategy. You need to know what you are going to ask and how you're going to ask it. You need to ask yourself a few pre-work questions. The first set of four pre-work questions will help you determine where you need to ask questions.

What part of my organization knows me best?

What part of my organization knows me least?

What parts of my organization remain a mystery to me?

What part of my organization is most critical to our success?

Then ask yourself how you're going to start to be a leader who asks questions.

How will I explain my new behavior to people?

How will I use the answers I receive?

How will I deal with answers I don't want to hear?

How will I start asking more questions?

With these questions answered, map out your plan. Maybe you're a question-of-the-week kind of person. Your style could include a general announcement that you are adopting a different approach and would appreciate support and feedback on your efforts. You could just quietly start asking. Use the worksheets at the end of each chapter. They are designed to help you find your own questions to ask and answer. You might want to enlist the aid of a trusted confidant. Let them in on your plans and ask them to listen for comments from your team and give you feedback on peoples' reactions. Give yourself permission to focus on the doing rather than on perfection as you start. Better the hesitantly asked question than the never asked question.

All this planning aside, please understand that this book is more about your leadership journey and why asking questions will be an important part of it than it is about giving you a set of right answers. It is not my intent to prescribe the right time or the right place to ask or answer a question. This is not so much a book about how— how is external. It is about why. I am challenging you to move, as Peter Block suggests in *The Answer to How is Yes*, from *how and what works* to *why* and *what matters*.

I believe that you'd rather be a good leader than a poor one and that being a great leader would be even better. This book will help you wherever you are on your journey as a leader—if you are willing to take some risks, practice some new skills, and endure the discomfort of change. As you read, make sure you have a pen handy and take lots of notes. Transform the questions into your own words. Use these questions as springboards to create your own list. But, most of all, ask them! You'll be rewarded by the answers.

A Warning

Asking questions and absorbing the answers those questions elicit will take time, and time is often in short supply for a leader. Announcing orders is an efficient system that can save a leader time. And those pronouncements are appropriate—in a time of crisis or when basic information needs to be shared quickly. Many leaders fall into the trap of seeing everything as a crisis or an information dump to save themselves precious time. Be honest with yourself.

If everything is a crisis in your organization, or if you're stuck in the fantasy that it's the leader's job to tell most of the time, you need to reconsider your leadership strategy.

Convinced? Ready to go forth and ask? One thing to keep in mind: If you haven't been known as an up-close-and-personal type of leader, or if your culture has a history of strong hierarchies, don't be surprised if your questions are met with puzzled looks and long

> **You ask questions and pretty soon, you come up with answers.**
>
> —Theodore Leavitt,
> American marketing guru

silences. The looks and silences are a result of people doing an internal data search, trying to determine why you're asking, and what the consequences of an honest answer will be. Be prepared to wait and persist. People will almost always answer a question if you give them a pause long enough to do the processing they need to formulate an answer. Persistent questioning behavior will almost always result in an increase of the thoughtfulness, the depth, and the honesty of the answers you receive.

Speaking of answers, be prepared to listen and to get some answers you're not happy to hear. The truth, while important in the long term, can be painful in the short term. The worst thing you can do when faced with an uncomfortable answer is to get defensive and respond with a list of reasons explaining why something can't possibly be changed, why the answerer is obviously misinformed, or how this particular issue isn't your responsibility. Your job is to listen, really listen, and thank the answerer for their perspective.

acknowledgments

When you make your living as a speaker, writing a book is an especially lonely endeavor. After thinking you're writing alone for a while, you suddenly realize that there are whole audiences of people hovering around your computer as you type:

My family, who whispered words of encouragement when I got tired and frustrated (which often happened at the same time) and who wouldn't let me quit. Thanks to Frank, Paul, Dee, and Quinn, Miriam, and John.

My colleagues from the National Speakers Association (You should hire every one of them or at least buy their books.), who shared their own book-writing adventures when we were together and sent good wishes and inspiration when we weren't. Special thanks to those who actually watched me typing away when I should have been in a meeting: C. Leslie Charles, Lenora Billings-Harris, and Kathy Dempsey.

The people who know how to make books. Thanks to Jeff Herman who reads what I send him, sells it, and makes it all look easy. Thanks to Adrienne Hickey and her team at AMACOM who prodded and questioned to make this a better book—always thinking of you the reader.

My clients. After doing this work for more than eighteen years, there have been many of them. You were all crowded in my office with suggestions for stories and strategies. Many of these questions came while we were talking. I hope you all find your influence on these pages because I could never have done it without you.

answers, you want answers

THE GOAL OF asking questions is to get answers. Leaders ask questions to gather information, understand motivations, and uncover problems. Questions asked and answered in the workplace can uncover emotions, discover new approaches, and increase efficiency. All these desirable outcomes assume one thing—someone actually got answers to the questions they asked. You see, asking a question doesn't guarantee an answer. Life doesn't unfold like a TV courtroom drama. You remember the scene. The lawyer asks the guilty party a tough question. There's a pause—a long pause. The lawyer looks at the judge; the judge bangs the gavel and sternly says to the witness, "You are instructed to answer the question." The witness, properly admonished, takes a deep breath and confesses all. That's the fictionalized version of how questions work.

In the real world, there is no judge to compel an answer. Getting good answers to questions is left to the skill of the questioner. There are five behaviors you need to master to increase the quality and quantity of the answers you receive.

1. *Ask one question at a time.* Inexperienced questioners often fall into the trap of asking a flurry of questions all at once. Usually this happens because the questioner hasn't thought through the question they want to ask. Listen in. "Sarah, I was wondering what issues customers have been raising lately? I mean, why is a call is escalated to you? Is that new policy we instituted last week really having a negative effect?"

Poor Sarah. Which question is she supposed to answer? Bombardment happens because the questioner opened their mouth before they engaged their brain. A moment's reflection would have helped Sarah's leader realize that what they really wanted to know was the effect of the new policy. "Sarah, what customer reactions have you seen regarding the new policy we instituted last week?" This is a straightforward, unbiased question that Sarah could feel comfortable answering.

2. *Pause at the end of a question.* Make it long enough for the answerer to think, formulate, and deliver their answer. Silence is often overlooked as a leadership tool; when it

comes to asking questions, developing the skill of keeping your mouth shut is essential. Successful sales people have known the value of silence for years: *The first person who speaks after the question is asked—loses.* In the context of leaders asking questions, losing means the leader doesn't get an answer, doesn't get a good answer, or doesn't get the real answer.

Staying silent after asking a question involves more than just not talking. It means keeping eye contact, staying still, and feeling comfortable while you wait. (Okay, be honest. You're currently impatient, scanning the rest of the page, looking for the number that will indicate exactly how long you have to wait, right? Silence, even implied on the printed page, can make a leader nervous.) This very desirable behavior takes practice. Most people believe that they pause a sufficient length of time after they ask a question, but observation belies that. Pauses of two to three seconds are long if you've asked the question and fleeting if you're preparing an answer. Monitor both your own pauses after a question and your comfort with silence in any situation. Work your way up to at least a ten-second pause after a question and watch the quality of the answers you receive improve greatly.

3. ***Learn about listening.*** Not long ago, a participant walked into a session I was teaching on listening skills and asked if I would write his wife a note certifying he had passed the class. It seemed she had reviewed the conference brochure, noticed this class, and strongly suggested he attend. I replied that I would be happy to write her a note indicating

he had attended the class, but proving that he had learned something was up to him. Most of us haven't ever been taught to listen, been given feedback on our listening skills, or even spent any time thinking about how important good listening is. This would be a good time to do all three. I'm certain your human resources department can help you find a class; your spouse or significant other will give you feedback; and now that it has been brought up, you can figure out the consequences of bad listening on your own.

4. *Ask follow-up questions.* They distinguish a good interviewer from an average interviewer. We've all experienced the frustration of watching an interviewer ask a question, get an answer from the interviewee that begs for clarification, and then, rather than asking a follow-up question, simply move to the next question on their list. If you're like me, at that point you tune out the rest of the interview. Why? I believe that this behavior (not asking follow-up questions) sends a message to anyone who's listening, not to mention the person you're questioning, that you're just going through the motions. The questioner is obviously more interested in asking their questions than in getting the interviewee's answers.

When this behavior is exhibited by leaders, their employee's mental dialogue goes something like this: "Here we go again, probably went to another seminar on being a better leader, and this week we'll be subjected to a lot of silly questions. Probably has a quota of questions for the day. Doesn't care about the answers at all."

The one drawback of asking follow-up questions is that too many of them in a row starts to sound and feel like an interrogation. You can encourage clarification of points made in an answer by using verbal encouragers (formally called directed lead statements for those of you who want the technical term). You probably use them already during interesting conversations. "I didn't know that, tell me more." "What else happened?" "Did it happen again?" Although these are, in fact, questions, they are delivered without the upward inflection that is the verbal equivalent of a question mark. They are delivered with a flat end as a statement and will encourage further dialogue.

5. *Say thank you.* Your mother was right. Writing that thank-you note was important to the giver of the gift. No matter how often they said that thanks wasn't necessary, it was. Saying thank you to someone who's spent time helping you by answering your questions will increase the likelihood that you'll get more and deeper answers the next time you ask. And the way news travels in organizations, this thank-you behavior will enhance your reputation as a leader.

Consistently practicing these five behaviors will turn you into an effective questioner—one who gets answers. In the next chapter, you're going to be asking yourself some questions. You'll be able to practice these skills on yourself—focus on a single question, stop and think, listen to both the things you say and the things you feel after each question. Ask yourself follow-up questions to dig deeper, and give yourself a pat on the back for answering.

The Power and Problem of <u>Why</u>?

Why is it that adults who understand, on an intellectual level, the need for two- and three-year-olds to learn about the world around them by asking questions are driven crazy by the sound of yet another *Why?* I believe this frustration comes from the adult's resentment that the child didn't accept their first answer. Successful parents quickly learn that their child's *why* is an amazing entrée into the learning process. Children have to ask more *whys* because they're asking questions in order to understand, and that learning happens under the surface. Repeated *whys* push the answerer beyond the surface. *Why* takes them to the details they need to satisfy their curiosity. Notice that a child's *whys* will stop when they have enough information to satisfy their quest. A powerful result from asking a simple one-word question.

Repeatedly asking *why* of adults can have a different, less favorable result. An adult, when confronted with a barrage of *whys*, may feel as though their authority is being questioned, their reputation is being challenged, or their expertise is being doubted. This isn't a great way to start a dialogue. But *why* does get you under the surface, the place you need to go in order to solve problems, expose underlying issues, or uncover problematic attitudes. What's a leader to do?

Here are two suggestions for a leader to use *why* effectively. Discover the one that fits your situation best and practice.

1. Watch your tone of voice. The most common problem with the simple question *why* is the way it is asked. Try the following exercise. Close your office door or mutter under your breath so the people around you don't think you're

crazy, and ask the one word *why* with the following emotions behind each *why*.

Curiosity

Anger

Frustration

Search for knowledge

Innocence

Could you feel the difference? If you pay attention to the emotion that is driving your need to ask *why*, and if you control it properly, I think you'll be okay. You will get immediate feedback—the nonverbal reaction of the person you've asked—and that will help you monitor your skill in asking *why* in a positive, nonjudgmental way.

2. In a more formal setting, possibly a team meeting, use the *Five Whys* technique made famous during business's focus on quality. Asking *why* five times in a more formal process with Post-it notes and flipcharts takes much of the accusatory nature out of the *why* process. The technique is fairly simple. Decide on the issue you need to explore and put it on a flipchart. Together with your team, ask *why*. You will probably get several different answers to that first *why*. Put each answer on a flipchart and explore four more *whys* for each of the original answers. Your intent in this process is to get to the root cause of the issue. By the way, the

flipcharts are optional. A legal pad works just as well. The intent of this process is to remove any feeling of attack or confrontation.

Just because asking *why* can be difficult doesn't mean it shouldn't be asked. Leaders need to discover the ways they can ask *why* with a spirit of curiosity and learning. Asking *why* is a basic skill that all leaders need to master. Think about how you can use *why* effectively. After asking *why* for a while, you'll be motivated to ask the other questions in this book.

chapter 1

questions leaders need to ask themselves

BEFORE YOU prepare to go forth and ask questions of others, you need to ask yourself a few questions. Don't skip this step because if you do, the questions you ask others will ring false. Leaders who have decided to go beneath the surface of their relationships with the people they lead need to start by being honest with themselves.

A client asked me when I thought they should start training people for leadership positions. "What are you doing now?" I asked innocently. "We don't have any formal leadership training right now," she replied without any trace of concern. I believe that most of us agree that leadership is both an art and a science. Unfortunately, most organizations that promote people into leadership positions, like hers, teach neither.

Maybe that's what happened to you. You were promoted to a position that required you to supervise others because you were good at doing the tasks they do. You learned leadership by trial and

> **One who never asks either knows everything or nothing.**
> —Malcom Forbes, American publisher

error, finding yourself doing and saying the things your bosses did and said to you. The very things that, when they were done to you, made you promise yourself you'd never do to anyone else. You're reading this book because you have lived with the uncomfortable feeling that you're not living up to your potential as a leader. Good for you. So here's your first assignment. Read through this chapter and answer the questions yourself. It will take some time, but there will be an enormous payoff for your efforts.

■ ■ ■

1. What does leadership mean?

Believe it or not, there isn't a right or wrong answer to this question. Leadership takes on different meanings depending on the person who leads and the people being led. On any given day, leadership can mean teaching, coaching, assigning, cheerleading, counseling, guiding, correcting, protecting, explaining, and observing. Leadership asks you to fill out forms, chair meetings, hold hands, explain decisions, think about the future, and resolve conflict. None of these actions or tasks will happen discretely; usually they'll happen all at once. If you thought becoming the boss would give you more control of your time and tasks, think again. Like the new entrepreneur, you'll discover that you have less control over your daily activities as you work to help and support the people you lead.

The trap I see new leaders fall into most often is the inability to see that their work has fundamentally changed. Since leaders are typically promoted because of their technical skills in an area—they were really good at dealing with customers so they were promoted to lead others who interact with customers—it is predictable that the new leader will continue to practice the skills that got them the promotion rather than understand that they have a whole new skill set to develop. No one has explained that their primary responsibility has shifted from doing to helping others do.

Since so few organizations provide the forum for discussing and learning leadership skills, you're going to have to have the discussion with and for yourself. Start by asking yourself what leadership means. Review your opinions of those who led you in the past. What did you admire about their behaviors? What behaviors did they exhibit that actually got in the way of your doing your job?

Identify the best leader you know inside your organization and invite them to lunch. Ask them to describe their view of leadership and how they developed it. Then, seek the company of a leader you admire outside your organization and ask them the same questions. Compare the responses. You might be surprised by how much the culture of an organization influences perceptions about leadership. If you have the time and opportunity, have this same discussion with a few additional leaders. But, make sure you do at least two.

After your research is done, go back to the original question, *What does leadership mean?* and answer it for yourself. This is a pencil and paper answer. Write your own definition of leadership and post it where you can see in it your office, put it on the back of one of your business cards and carry it in your wallet, and make it the screensaver on your computer. Just don't chisel it into stone. As you grow into your role as a leader, you'll probably want to revise your definition. Not because your first answer was wrong, but because your later answers will be better for the experience you've gained.

2. How do you feel about being a leader?

When you got the message that you were being promoted into a leadership position, I'd guess you were excited. Promotions usually mean more prestige, more opportunities, and more money. People congratulate you, offer to buy you lunch, and your picture appears in the company newsletter. Good news all the way around.

Then there's the reality. Tasks are dumped on your desk with little or no explanation attached. People are clamoring for your time and attention. Meetings on subjects you've never heard of fill your schedule. Those who report to you expect you to solve their problems, resolve their conflicts, and even deliver feedback messages they're too afraid to deliver themselves. It's time to think about your feelings.

Leadership is more than a skill set. Real leadership is a combination of well-honed skills combined with an open and gracious spirit. How you feel about being a leader will always influence how you act as a leader. People who believe that leadership is their right, who believe that their title demands the respect of others, or who believe that leaders should always have the final say are carrying feelings about leadership that will constantly get in the way of their effectiveness as a leader. Closemindedness is usually a result of an unwillingness to explore the feeling side of an issue. How are you at exploring your feelings about being a leader?

It's perfectly okay to have conflicting emotions about being a leader. Excitement mixed with apprehension. Confidence colored by fear. Certainty alongside doubt. Pride with anger. It's not about *either/or*, it's about *and*. Leaders who identify all the emotions that can go along with leadership, study the full range of those emotions, and learn to tap into the appropriate emotion for the right situation are ahead of the game. Leaders who try to convince themselves that dealing with emotions (their own as well as those of others) isn't part of their job are just kidding themselves.

So, how do you feel about being a leader? Like the previous question, your answer to this question will change with time and experience. In this case, feelings being what they are, your answer might be different from one minute to the next. That's not the big problem. Understanding how your feelings at any given time are influencing your behavior is one of the greatest challenges of leadership. Without an honest, routine check of your feelings about leadership, you shortchange yourself as well as the people who follow you.

■ ■ ■

3. What do you want to be remembered for?

When my daughter, Miriam, went to college in Milwaukee, she worked at a bakery. Vann's Pastry Shop was legendary for its specialty cakes, Danish pastries, and bread. When Mr. Vann died, his obituary in the *Milwaukee Journal Sentinel* started with the following: "Calling Bob Vann a baker would be like calling Frank Lloyd Wright an architect." When you die and someone puts their fingers on a keyboard, ready to write about you as a leader, what do you hope they'll type?

There is a philosophy that says you should always start with the end in mind. An obituary is definitely an end, and I'm certainly not suggesting that it's the end you need to have in mind in order to answer this question. But what about asking yourself, "When I move to another position, what do I want my team to say about me as a leader? What do I want to be remembered for?"

Create a list of characteristics you admire in a leader. The combinations are endless. Compassionate and a great listener. Creative and fair-minded. Uplifting and supportive. Enthusiastic and knowledge-

> When you stop learning, stop listening, stop looking and asking questions, always new questions, then it is time to die.
> —Lillian Smith, American author

able. After you've identified at least fifteen characteristics, highlight five of them. Are these the five you'd be happy to have people use to describe you? Keep working your list until you're convinced that you have the five you believe are the cornerstones of your leadership style.

Now, think of your leadership actions over the last week. Did you devote your time to these behaviors? If this had been your last week as a leader for this team, how would they describe your final days as their leader? It isn't enough to identify, think about, or even talk about the things you want to be remembered for. It's only how you act that will count in the end.

Mr. Vann was a baker, but he was so much more than that. I asked Miriam what she remembered about him after we read the obituary. She said he taught her that discipline is required to produce a consistently superior product, that working as a team can be fun, and that finding out what you are good at is important in life and work. A very nice legacy for any leader.

■ ■ ■

4. Are you happy?

Let me admit it right up front—this is a bias. I believe that fundamentally unhappy people make poor leaders. This statement might cause you to pause. If we were having a conversation, I'd be able to see your reaction in your eyes, and I'd repeat myself for emphasis. So let me repeat. I believe that fundamentally unhappy people make poor leaders.

In an age of cynicism, the importance of happiness as a key part of the human condition gets lost or overlooked. Young children are envied for their happiness, but it is credited to their ignorance of the world's harsh realities. "It's easy for them," we say. "They don't have a care in the world. Oh, to be like that again. I know too much to go around happy all the time." I'm willing to admit that there is some truth in that statement. Sometimes ignorance makes it easier to be happy, but the opposite isn't true. You don't have to be ignorant in order to be happy. What so many people seem to lose sight of is that happiness, much like ignorance, isn't a state, it is a choice. If you are ignorant, you can choose to get smarter. If you are unhappy, you can choose to become happy. Choosing happiness doesn't mean that you banish all concerns and troubles. Happiness simply means that you understand all the sides of an issue, good and bad, and choose to be happy anyway.

What, you may be asking, does this have to do with leadership? Everything, I think. Happiness is born from optimism. Optimism is embedded in beliefs such as "Problems can be solved," "Good ultimately triumphs over evil," and "Joy is a birthright of all individuals." Without an underlying positive belief system, leadership rings hollow. You cannot inspire people to try again if you don't really believe that success is possible. You can't comfort people during tough times if you don't believe that tough times pass. You can't lead if you don't have faith in an uncertain future.

So, are you happy? Don't worry if your answer is no. You can choose a different answer when you ask yourself the question again, and then get to work to make your answer true. The people around you will be glad you gave this question a second look.

■ ■ ■

5. What are you afraid of?

Fear is a powerful emotion. It can paralyze you in times of crisis, cause you to cower in the face of an adversary, or lash out in an inappropriate direction. Fear will keep you silent when you should speak. Fear will open your mouth when it's better left shut. And, worst of all for a leader, fear will convince you to back off and hide just when you need to be most visible.

You don't, however, need to eliminate fear in order to be a leader. If that were the case, only idiots could become leaders. Fear, in addition to being a powerful emotion, is a necessary one. Rational fears

---

I go with what scares me.

—American actor Helen Hunt
on choosing roles

---

cause us to think carefully and research diligently before we invest large sums of money in a project. Intelligent fears propel us to have a tough conversation before promoting a marginal job candidate. Gut-level fears remind us to forgo a walk on a dark street in an unfamiliar neighborhood. Eliminating any of these fears would be just plain stupid. Think about fear this way—you just need to make sure you control fear rather than letting fear control you.

If you approach leadership with a great deal of fear, your behavior will be influenced. If you're afraid that you've been promoted beyond your competency, you'll be hesitant to ask questions that might show your ignorance. If you're afraid that people think you don't deserve to be a leader, you'll avoid necessary confrontations. If you're afraid to make a wrong decision, you'll second-guess yourself into a really bad decision or, even worse, make no decision at all.

A leader's fears must be self-diagnosed. You need to spend time thinking about what you fear. Your task isn't to search out your fears in order to eliminate them. Your job is to think through how those fears might influence your leadership behaviors. You might want to discuss your conclusions with a trusted advisor in order to get a fresh perspective on how fear might be influencing your actions.

Don't let fear get in the way of your development as a leader. *What am I afraid of?* is an important question to ask yourself and an even more important question to answer honestly. Don't let fear keep you from doing just that.

■ ■ ■

6. Are you sure you want to ask questions?

As with any new endeavor, starting is the hardest part. Reasons to postpone action exist in abundance. "I'll start after I finish reading the book." "Mondays are better for beginnings than Thursdays." Even traumatic events that would appear to cry out for changed behavior (the heart attack victim who smokes, the parent whose child gets picked up by the police for a minor offense, the leader who loses three key employees in a short period of time) don't always have the desired effect. Smokers still smoke. Parents ignore early warning signs of a troubled child. Leaders blame the competition for stealing away their people. Behavior doesn't change and problems escalate.

There is a simple, common, clever definition of insanity going around: *Insanity is doing the same thing, in the same way, while expecting different results.* I've seen many leaders who, by this definition, are insane. Some are even proud of their unchanging behavior, believing that sooner or later they'll get people on their team who will appreciate their leadership style for the success it is supposed to be. While these leaders are waiting for this fantasy day to arrive, real leaders are constantly challenging themselves to try something different, learn something smarter, and risk something deeper.

Real leaders are brave. They're willing to say, "I don't know it all." They ask for opinions, help, and guidance. They change. They fail. They discard what doesn't work, question the status quo, and keep well-working traditions alive. They look at themselves in the mirror and see their reflection honestly. They think. They take action. They persist and persevere. They are gentle with themselves as they learn and stern with themselves when they think about giving up. They ask questions.

What about you? Are you brave enough to venture forward on this journey? Are you certain that you want to ask questions? No one can answer this one but you. You can't seek the recommendations of others. Either you will or you won't. Either you do or you don't. Reading this book won't make it happen; thinking about, absorbing, and acting on the ideas in this book will. But, in the end, it's up to you. Your answer and your questions.

■ ■ ■

▮ ▮ ▮ ▮ ▮ ▮ ▮ ▮ ▮ **WHAT DID YOU LEARN?** ▮ ▮ ▮ ▮ ▮ ▮ ▮ ▮ ▮ ▮

The questions in this chapter were designed to be tough. Were they? If you took them seriously, they were. They required that you think deeply, honestly, and thoroughly. An easy answer given to any of them means you should go back and rethink your conclusions. Being willing to answer tough questions you pose to yourself allows you the right to ask tough questions of others.

By asking and answering the various questions, you've begun to frame your own view of leadership. You now have challenges to confront, measures of success to monitor, and actions to take. Use the

> **The only questions that really matter are the ones you ask yourself.**
>
> —Ursula K. LeGuin, American writer

worksheets in this book (you'll find them at the end of each chapter) to reflect upon the lessons you learned from asking and answering these questions.

Because you've gone through this self-evaluation process, you're ready to take the next step. Read on.

▮ ▮ ▮ ▮ ▮ ▮ ▮ ▮ ▮ **CHAPTER ONE WORKSHEET** ▮ ▮ ▮ ▮ ▮ ▮ ▮ ▮ ▮ ▮

1. Which of the questions in this chapter did you find the most challenging? Why?

_____

_____

_____

_____

_____

_____

_____

2. Which question in this chapter did you have the most fun answering? Why?

_____

_____

_____

_____

_____

_____

_____

3. What other questions did this chapter make you think of?

_____

_____

_____

_____

_____

_____

4. How would you answer those questions?

_____

_____

_____

_____

_____

_____

_____

5. What is the one thing you want to remember most from this chapter?

_____

_____

_____

_____

_____

_____

_____

6. What leadership ideas do you want to explore further?

_____

_____

_____

OTHER NOTES

---

chapter 2

questions leaders need to ask customers

HAVE YOU ever had an unsatisfactory conversation with a customer service representative? One of those situations where you felt the person didn't care, couldn't do anything to fix the problem, or that the person's answer couldn't be trusted? Several years ago I had a particularly bad experience with an American Airlines customer service representative. I asked for and was transferred to a supervisor, and together we worked out a solution to the problem that had prompted my call in the first place. We wrapped up our conversation, and she repeated her apology for the way I had been treated.

I explained that I appreciated her words and hoped that my upcoming trip on her airline would help erase the lingering concerns I had about doing business with American Airlines. As I hung up the phone, I turned to my husband, Frank, and said, "If she's smart, I'll have an upgrade when I check in for my flight tomorrow." "Yeah, right," he replied.

Most women hate to admit when their husbands are right. Frank was. I took my flight—in coach. It was okay, as was my return trip. Not good or bad, just okay. I got home three days later and found a soggy box on the front porch. It had been delivered while both of us were out of town and left to the mercies of the northern Wisconsin late fall weather. Dumping the dripping box into the basement sink, I opened it to find ruined pastries with a note of apology from the American Airlines supervisor. I don't think I've flown American since.

I'm tempted to make this a quiz. How many customer service problems can you find in this story? For now, I'm willing to skip the unreliable package delivery process, the fact that she knew I was going to be away from my home, and the absurdity of an airline sending baked goods, and go right to what I believe is the most telling part of the story. She never asked me the best and simplest customer service recovery question ever conceived: *What can we do to make you feel happy about doing business with us again?* My answer would have been "Upgrade me." With a few keystrokes she'd have been done, and I would be writing a different, happier story for you to read. No requisition for baked goods, no delivery form to fill out, no subtract-it-from-the-bottom-line expense, and no waste of her time.

This isn't a book about customer service. It's a book about questions and answers. Did you get the point? A well-placed question to a customer and a questioner who listens well to the answer can, in itself, be a great customer service strategy. It can also be a great place for leaders to begin practicing their questioning skills. Leaders who do not look for opportunities to interact with a wide cross section of their customers will pay a price for this ignorance. In this chapter, you will find questions you can use as you take advantage of customer interactions. While we're on the subject of asking questions

> **Not to know is bad; not to wish to know is worse.**
> —Nigerian proverb

of your customers, let me remind you of the warning I issued earlier in this book. Listening to the answers to your questions, especially when it's your customer you're listening to, requires skill. Take a deep breath and really listen. Listen to more than the words. Don't be defensive and give in to the natural impulse to explain away the negative comments you hear. Accept your customer's comments in the spirit in which they're offered and don't forget to say *thank you*.

By the way, if you happen to work for American Airlines and would like to practice your questioning skills, please feel free to give me a call.

7. Why do you do business with us?

Remember the song from *Fiddler on the Roof* when Tevye asks his wife of many years, "Do you love me?" It's a wonderful moment, and you can tell couples who have been together for a long time by their behavior during that scene. They poke each other, grin, hold hands, or mouth, "Well, do you?" There's a lesson for business in that song.

Do you know why your customers buy goods and services from you? Do they love you? Asking this question will help you find out. Asking this question and analyzing the results will provide you with a foundation of information that will help you formulate your strategy. When a leader takes the time to talk to customers, both external and internal, relationships are built. When a leader goes beyond talking to a well-crafted and well-executed questioning strategy, long-term customer partnerships can happen.

If a customer joins Tevye in singing of their love for your location, hours of operation, products and services, or your innovation and design, you've uncovered a champion. If your customer says their loyalty isn't to your products but to an individual in your organization, you've learned something different. If they confess that they do business with you grudgingly and are waiting for someone else to introduce a similar product and service so they can buy from them, you've uncovered a problem. No matter how your question gets answered, you now know things you didn't know before.

Asking your customers this question and those that follow gets you immediate feedback and insight into your future. Some of the answers might make you uncomfortable; all of them will provide you and your organization opportunities to improve and grow. You will hear reasons to celebrate, reasons to make changes, and reasons to re-examine your policies and procedures. You'll have work to do.

8. Why do you do business with our competition?

This is the flip side of the last question. By asking this question, you're seeking information that will allow you to compare and contrast your customer's opinion of you and your competition.

I don't know any business or organization that doesn't have competition. I don't know any business or organization that doesn't need to know more about their competition. It seems to me that asking your customers about your competition is an obvious place to start learning. Your view of your competition is inherently biased. You have preconceived notions of your superiority of product, your extraordinary customer service response, and your exceptionally speedy customer responsiveness. If you didn't, you wouldn't be working there, leading a team, right? Having a positive mental image of your organization is good as long as it is tested against your customers' opinions on a regular basis.

It occurs to me that fear might stop you from asking this question. What if you found out that your competition was really doing a good job? What if your customer confided that they were switching to your competition? Think of it this way: What if your customer was thinking those things and you didn't know about them? Without the information gained by asking this question, you have no chance to change things for the better. Shouldn't you be more afraid of that?

You may lead in an organization that is fortunate enough and big enough to have entire departments that measure customer opinions. That doesn't replace the value of hearing those opinions for yourself. Asking your customers questions about your competition will help you understand the reports that land on your desk in a deeper way. You may lead in a small organization where decisions are more often made by hunch than by research. Your quest to listen to your customers' opinions of your competition is even more important. This information can provide valuable insights into your customers' behavior in the future.

Finally, asking a customer this question might spark the awareness that you really care about their opinion. Certainly it will help them understand how much you value them as a customer.

■ ■ ■

9. How and when have we made it hard for you to do business with us?

Not many organizations choose to have conferences and hold meetings where I live in northern Wisconsin. (Maybe our annual snowfall has something to do with that decision.) That means that, to do my work, I need to travel. When you stay in hotels often, you sign your name frequently. Check-in. Check-out. Room service bills. Bar tabs. Snack from the gift shop. Each form has three lines, one for your room number, one for your signature and one for the PRINT YOUR NAME command. The other day I realized that, because I paid attention in penmanship class, my signature is perfectly legible. So I declined to follow the PRINT YOUR NAME command. The server who picked up my check noticed this omission and asked, nicely, if I would *print my name*. "Why," I replied, "since my signature is perfectly readable?" "Because you have to," he announced. "Not necessary," I answered. "I'll have to call the manager," he said. "Give the check back to me," I demanded. With the offending charge slip back in my hands and tempted to lower his tip, I scribbled my name illegibly in the heavily disputed PRINT YOUR NAME space. Why, if my handwriting is a nonissue when I pay for a meal in the hotel's restaurant directly with my MasterCard, does it become a matter of state security when I want to charge something to the hotel bill that will eventually be settled with the aforementioned MasterCard? Not a big deal, but enough of an annoyance to encourage me to find a restaurant outside the hotel for dinner the next time.

Your customers never encounter a policy or procedure problem when they do business with you, right? When was the last time you checked? Every business needs systems, policies, and procedures to function. Employees need to understand their jobs, the technologies that support their work, and the boundaries that limit their authority. Leaders need to deliver decisions in context, envision opportunities for the future, and watch budgets. Where is the voice of the customer heard? Internal systems are seldom viewed from the outside, and until they are, you can't call yourself customer-friendly.

The only way to understand how your systems and processes feel is to ask a customer. Just as it is impossible to proofread something you've written, it is impossible to judge your own systems with a clear eye. Asking this question of lots of customers can be an eye-opening experience, and the answers might provide some clear directions for changes that need to be made to your policies. Making things hard for your customers, even when it's by accident, isn't a good idea.

■ ■ ■

10. What will you need from us in the future?

I remember one of my earliest business conversations involved the kitchen table, my father, and a company called International Business Machines. I was about eleven. Dad was telling us that his company had gotten a contract to make a part for IBM, but his team didn't know anything about the product the parts were going to be used in. Even at eleven that didn't make much sense. "How," I asked, "can you tell if what you're making is right?" "We can't," my Dad replied. "We just wait for them to tell us how close we are to getting it right and then we do it over again."

This is the partnership question. Leaders who want to deepen their relationships with their customers ask this question often. In fact, it quickly becomes one of their favorite questions to ask. Understanding your customer's view of their future helps you get a glimpse of your future. Asking this question will get you lots of data. First, there's the basic information. Information that will give you insights into how you'll have to innovate or modify your processes and products to meet your customer's need in the future. Customers who can't articulate their view of the future may not be a long-term asset for you.

Next, you can judge the excitement level. The future is a funny thing. People and organizations that are excited about the future generally have a promising future. People who are pessimistic about the future often face bleaker times. Who would you rather have on your client list?

When you combine the quality of the information you get from the customer with the enthusiasm level generated by giving the answer, you've got impressive insight into your own crystal ball. Targeting those customers who think and plan for the future and are excited about the possibilities the future hold for them seems like a great way to plan your future success. These are the customers you'd like to partner with. But you'll never know who they are unless you ask the question.

■ ▓ ▊

11. If you were me, what's one thing you'd change about my organization?

This question is designed to take the conversation to the level of specific action. This is the *What would make us better?* question, with teeth. You're asking your customer to express the thoughts and ideas they had while waiting on hold, fighting to get an invoice corrected, or shaking their head over one of your policies. You're asking your customer to tell you the truth, and that's a big deal. An even bigger deal is what you do with the answer to this question. Listening and asking for clarification are acceptable responses. Explaining why you can't or won't try the suggestion isn't.

A note of caution. If you ask a customer this question about change, don't be surprised if your customer asks it back at you. What would you say? And if this original question-and-answer session turns into an ongoing dialogue, you may find yourself facing a partnership waiting to happen.

Actually, you'll have better luck asking this question of a customer who considers you a partner rather than a vendor. As the world of business has gotten more complex, customers are looking for the opportunity to work with their suppliers instead of just buying from them. Working together in a partnership relationship, seeing the world from a broader viewpoint than either one of you could ever envision on your own, allows both parties to gain. These partnerships go beyond the traditional working toward a win/win situation. They exist to create. Create new ways of going to market, new ways to solve problems, and new ways to define success.

Partnership carries with it the desire for two-way feedback. In fact, the only way partnerships work is when both parties are willing to make the commitment to a continuous stream of feedback—what's working and what's not. Terry McElroy from McLane Company is quoted in *Dance Lessons: Six Steps to Great Partnerships in Business & Life* by Chip Bell and Heather Shea as saying, "We are constantly asking ourselves, 'Are we doing business at the level we want to? Are we worthy of this partnership?' And we want partnerships with people who ask themselves those same questions." Another set of good questions.

12. How can we effectively tell you that we're grateful for your business?

This may be hard for male readers to understand, but when a woman moves, finding a skilled hairdresser is a critical, top-of-the-to-do-list task. When I moved to northern Wisconsin, I asked for recommendations, made appointments with several of those people, and chose one to be my official haircutter. Over the years that she cut and styled my hair, I never had a bad hair day. When I'd mention that I knew someone who was moving into town, or someone who wanted a new look, she'd hand me a card that offered 10 percent off their first visit. I counted. Over the ten years I went to this hairdresser I brought her twelve customers—all of whom visited her at least once a month. (You do the math.)

On the day that I had a hair emergency and she couldn't fit me into her schedule, I started thinking. How come she was rewarding the new customers I was recruiting for her and I wasn't getting any reward? Why wasn't I worthy of even some consideration for an emergency appointment? It was the beginning of the end of our client/hairdresser relationship. (Have you ever noticed how quickly resentment can build?) It didn't take me very long to find someone else who solved my bad-hair-day situation. The next month, as my possible replacement hairdresser cut my hair, I mentioned it was my birthday that week. "Oh," she said. "You're in luck. I give my clients a 50 percent discount on their birthdays." Guess who has been cutting my hair for the last ten years.

Showing that you're grateful doesn't always involve giving something of monetary value. Businesses that express their gratitude do so in many ways. They use their customer's names—all the time. They keep track of preferences and make suggestions that solve problems. They send cards on days without a holiday attached. They make eye contact and listen. They anticipate. They're creative. They fall in love with their customers and show it.

How do you reward your clients? Often, in an attempt to build new business, we forget to value the business and clients we already have. Asking how to show gratitude is key to avoiding that trap. Not only will you hear about ways to say *thank you*, you'll discover which *thank yous* are most meaningful for your customers.

■ ■ ■

▌ ▌ ▌ ▌ ▌ ▌ ▌ ▌ ▌ **WHAT DID YOU LEARN?** ▌ ▌ ▌ ▌ ▌ ▌ ▌ ▌ ▌ ▌

Learning when and how to ask questions of your customers is where you begin because asking questions of your customers is a good habit for leaders to develop. Spending time listening to your customers is an even better one. In many organizations, people go to great lengths to keep their leaders insulated from the customer. Nothing should be further from the reality for a leader who wants to deserve the title of leader.

Keeping close to a cross section of your customers is a key activity of a leader. Quick phone calls, meals with key customers, and face-to-face meetings with major clients are just a few of the ways

> **The real questions are the ones that intrude upon your consciousness whether you like it or not.**
>
> —Ingrid Bengis, American writer

customer-focused leaders stay in contact with the people who make their businesses possible. Not doing these things feels way too risky for them. Contrary to the old saying, "No news isn't good news… it's just no news."

Leaders know better than to face the future with no news. Crafting your questions before you connect with your customers is the best habit of all.

▮ ▮ ▮ ▮ ▮ ▮ ▮ ▮ ▮ **CHAPTER TWO WORKSHEET** ▮ ▮ ▮ ▮ ▮ ▮ ▮ ▮ ▮ ▮

1. Which of the questions in this chapter would you have the most difficulty asking? Why?

_____

_____

_____

_____

_____

_____

2. What strategies do you use to stay personally close to your customers?

_____

_____

_____

_____

_____

_____

3. What other questions would you like to ask your customers?

_____

_____

_____

_____

4. How could you ask these questions?

5. What questions do your customers ask you?

6. How did you answer them?

_____

_____

_____

7. What is the one thing you want to remember most from this chapter?

_____

_____

_____

_____

_____

_____

_____

OTHER NOTES

_____

_____

_____

_____

_____

_____

_____

chapter 3

questions leaders need to ask employees about the business

SO FAR, you've been considering asking questions of yourself and your customers. Important work to be sure, but as a leader, you also need to focus your attention on the people you lead. Asking questions of them is the core of this book.

The easiest and best place to focus your early questions for your employees is around the business. It's amazing how many well-educated, fairly successful employees know a lot about their area of responsibility and virtually nothing about what goes on in the department down the hall. IT people don't understand the salespeoples' challenges. Marketing types take mental vacations when profit and loss statements are discussed. The packer in the shipping department doesn't even realize the company has a research department.

One of my favorite questions to ask a new client is "Do you give tours of your organization to outside groups?" When the answer is yes, I follow it up with "Is that tour, in greater depth, part of your new employee orientation program?" We're not even going

> Leaders, by their openness to questioning, give followers the confidence to pursue their dreams.
>
> —Andrew Finlayson,
> American author and journalist

to talk about the number of people who stare blankly at the mention of an employee orientation program, but a yes to the second question is fairly uncommon. That being the case, I can only assume that there are many people working in organizations without a clear understanding of the business they're in. That feels risky to me. What's a leader to do? Asking the questions in this chapter is a logical place to start.

You'll ask these questions for two reasons. First, to understand the depth (or shallowness) of the knowledge people have about your organization as a whole. Second, to provide you with an opportunity to impart knowledge, correct misinformation, and encourage exploration—in other words, to adopt the role of teacher for a while. Teaching, in the non-classroom sense, is a major part of a leader's job, and these questions will provide you with the opening to play that role.

Caution: Teaching does not mean lecturing. Asking an employee one of these questions, getting a vague or confused answer, and proceeding to deliver an on-the-spot lecture in an authoritative tone will not get you the results you desire. Teaching means thinking about and delivering the information that the student needs in a way that will be meaningful to them. The answers to these questions may start a brief dialogue, a one-on-one walk through a department with narration, or an invitation to a representative from another department to a team meeting for an old-fashioned show-and-tell. The purpose of these questions is to help you discover what needs to happen next.

If this is your first real step into being a leader who asks questions, go back and read *A Warning* at the beginning of this book. There are a few things you need to think about before you burst out of your office looking for a poor unsuspecting employee to question. That section will help you remember what they are.

■ ■ ■

13. How do we make money?

A simple question. "We sell things." "We make things and sell them." "We publish books." If you work in a retail or manufacturing environment, those answers should be pretty obvious. What if you provide a service? "We help people solve problems." "We fix things that break." "We show movies." Surface answers all. Printing books, selling something, fixing someone's equipment allows an organization to present an invoice but does not ensure that anyone makes any money.

Most people have never been taught how business works, a fact that has fueled the Open-Book Management philosophy. In an article in the June 1995 issue of *Inc.*, John Case describes the three elements that make Open-Book Management different.

1. Every employee sees—and learns to understand—the company's financials, along with all the other numbers that are critical to tracking the business's performance.

2. Employees learn that, whatever else they do, part of their job is to move those numbers in the right direction.

3. Employees have a direct stake in the company's success.

Employees in an Open-Book Management organization know how their organization makes money. But, I can hear you saying, "We're not an Open-Book company and I don't have the authority to make us one. True. But you can do your homework by asking this question of the members of your team, evaluating the responses, and establishing a plan to help your team see the big picture when it comes to the bottom line.

This could be scary if it occurs to you that you don't actually know the answer to this question yourself. Don't use that as an excuse to not ask the question. Use it as a reason to ask it of someone who knows and learn from them.

∎   ∎   ∎

14. How does your work contribute to our success?

Years ago I was a salesperson for a large insurance company. Sitting in a client's office (an unhappy client's office) I asked to use the phone to call the home office to get the answer to his very pointed question. As I dialed our toll-free number, engaging in silent prayer as I pushed each button, it occurred to me that I hadn't ever used the main toll-free number before. It was picked up on the third ring and answered by a cheerful person who was chewing gum so loudly I could almost see her jaw working. I was so glad I had dialed rather than my client.

On the way back to my office, I envisioned the confrontation she and I were going to have. I was going to tell her, in no uncertain terms, how unprofessional her behavior was. Chewing gum into the ears of the hundreds of callers she must talk to in a day—what was she thinking? Since it was a thirty-mile drive back, I had time to think through my initial plan and found it lacking. I needed to talk to her leader. No one, it seemed to me, had helped her understand the importance of her job. When she answered the phone, she represented the entire organization to the person on the other end of the line. I was pretty certain that had never occurred to her. Her leader had never asked her how she envisioned her contribution to the success of the entire company.

As a leader, it is fundamental to your job that each person you lead, whether they're accountants or janitors, understands that they play a crucial part in your organization's success. If you don't know how to explain that, or worse, don't believe that statement is true, stop calling yourself a leader. It is the leader's job to create the context in which each member of their team does their work.

You need to explain it in the beginning, watch for understanding in the daily work, and reward it on a regular basis.

I talked to the receptionist's leader about the gum chewing. His blank-stare response helped me understand her behavior. I started telling my clients to call in directly to my administrative assistant when they needed to talk to someone in the company. She never chewed gum. I asked her lots of questions—this one on her first day.

■ ■ ■

15. How could we save money?

Back to the money stuff. Well, one could argue that most of business is about the money stuff, but asking about the money often gets you to something more valuable. This question does that. Leaders ask this question to investigate, challenge, and assign responsibility. They use it to investigate the forgotten areas within their control but not in their view, to challenge people to think for themselves, and to let people know that they are expected to engage their brains on the job.

Look at it this way. Pretend you don't do the grocery shopping in your household. In fact, you very seldom even go into a grocery store. The balance in your checking account is running lower than usual, and you notice that the checks made out to the grocery store represent a significant percentage of your monthly expenditures. So you sit down and develop a strategy to lower your grocery cost and present your plan to the family shopper for implementation. If you had to guess, how's that going to work for you?

Okay, try this approach. You catch the shopper as you walk through the kitchen and say, "You're spending way too much at the grocery store. I expect to see smaller checks in the future." And as you walk out of the room you add, "By the way don't let the quality of our meals suffer." Is that better?

Please tell me you didn't think that either of these approaches would work well. Please tell me that, as you read the last two paragraphs, you were shaking your head and grinning. Unfortunately, we act that way at home way too often. This behavior (as expressed about grocery shopping, punishment for children, and other areas too numerous to mention) has far-reaching implications—ask anyone you know who's gone through a divorce. Don't kid yourself. If you do it at home, you do it at work.

The problem with this behavior (in case you're not certain) is presuming that you know better than the person closest to the issue does. When you ask about saving the company money, you send a message that you expect and value your employees' expertise because they're the ones who do the work, day in and day out. Of course, the reasoning goes, they have ideas and I want—no, *need*— to hear them. The more you ask this question, the better the answers you get will be.

■ ■ ■

16. How could you make your job more effective?

I don't believe I've ever been asked this question. The closest I ever got was on a performance review form that had *Where do you see yourself in five years?* as the last question on the bottom of the last page. Silly me, I took it seriously. I thought about the work I was doing, the work I'd like to be doing, the problems and concerns expressed by our customers and developed a mini job description and envisioned myself in it. When my boss read it he said to me, "You can't want to want to do that." I could have handled a "You can't do that," answer, but I walked away from that performance review muttering, "You can't tell me what I want to do!"

What a different experience that would have been if he had only said, "This is an interesting proposal. What made you think of it?" I would have gladly shared the frustration—mine and my customers'—that made my job difficult. There were things he could have helped me do, right away, to become more effective and to make our clients happier, without creating a new job description.

Questions are powerful, and this is a great one. Issues that appear small from a leader's vantage point can be enormous barriers from the employee's. The people on your team may know what needs to happen to make their jobs more effective, but they may not know how to make the change. Helping someone think through those ideas and then, when appropriate, breaking down the barriers that hinder implementation, is a leader's job. But how can you break a barrier if you don't know it's there?

Ask this question more than once and you'll begin to see the quality of the thinking and the depth of caring about outcomes your people have. Working with them to eliminate the organizational barriers to trying these ideas will benefit you both.

17. What's the most important thing you know about our customers?

Every successful organization I've encountered, as a consultant or as a consumer, is passionate about their customers. When people in an organization hear their leaders at all levels talking about their customers at all times, it's easy for them to get the message that customers are important.

But talking about customers isn't enough. Ever notice how fast you can mentally turn someone off when you decide that what they're talking about doesn't apply to you? It's amazing to me how many people believe that if the words "customer service" aren't in their job description, customers aren't their responsibility. I decided recently that I wouldn't return to a particular restaurant because of misleading menu copy. The last complaint I heard about an e-business was over their packaging materials. Menu copywriters and purchasers of packaging materials are examples of people who may not realize that they are responsible for customer relationships. Leaders who ask questions about customers help people in all positions understand that learning the needs and wants of customers is everyone's job.

So, the questions you ask about customers direct, remind, and encourage your people to get and stay curious about your customers. The answers you get from your staff will provide a virtually unlimited supply of information to act on. Answers to this question will fall into four categories.

1. *People will not be able to answer.* Don't panic. This response tells you that you and your leadership team have some work to do. Some people will need to be reminded that they have a responsibility to understand their customers. Some people will need to learn the concept of serving internal customers.

Some people will need help to see how their work links to the work of others within the organization to ultimately serve your external customers.

2. *People's answers will be wrong.* Don't get mad. This is a perfect time for a follow-up question. *What leads you to believe this?* would be a good possibility. People may have been given incorrect information, may have jumped to a conclusion from a single encounter, or may be relying on old data. Helping people learn their customer responsibilities and fostering continued dialogue can clear up this misinformation.

3. *People's answers will confirm things you already know.* Don't get complacent. These responses, while comfortable, need to be looked at carefully. Do you really know your customers well or are you collectively operating on old data? Funny how one question leads to another, isn't it?

4. *People's answers will surprise you with insights you've never had.* Don't be embarrassed. These are the most exciting answers of all. Insights are a function of viewing the status quo with new eyes. If you lead an organization filled with people who consistently scan their environment, think about what they see, and draw insightful conclusions...well, things hardly get better than that!

18. What's something we could offer to our customers?

The best time to ask this question is when you're talking to a customer. The next best time to ask this question is when you're talking to someone on your team who regularly interacts with your customers. This is a question designed to generate ideas—lots of ideas from many sources. So your job with this question is to ask it of as many people as you can, as often as you can.

The worst possible position to be in when it comes to ideas is to have too few of them. That's why the primary rule of brainstorming is to amass quantity, not force quality. Unfortunately, many people forget this rule, ask for ideas, stifle the conversation by judging each idea as soon as it's mentioned, and then wonder why their people just don't brainstorm well. If you want to hear about ideas that might make your customers happy, you need to generate lots of ideas and consider them all—even the ones that are too costly, too time-consuming, or too outrageous.

Creativity is messy. The best ideas never appear fully formed and practical. They are often hidden inside an idea that is impractical and silly. These best ideas need to be coaxed, nurtured, and defended. Creating an environment that encourages creative thinking isn't always easy, but it's usually fun.

■ ■ ■

19. Who do you see as our competition, and what do you know about them?

The nature of my work requires that I spend a great deal of time away from home. Time alone in hotel rooms provides fertile ground for unusual questions to surface. One evening I got to wondering how a hotel concierge learns about the places they recommend. So I asked. I was amazed to discover that, for the most part, they are expected to learn about shops, restaurants, and local attractions on their own time with their own dollars. That got me thinking about how organizations learn about their competition.

(If this apparent leap in subject is uncomfortable for you, get used to it. Not because it is a fault of mine, but because it is a common occurrence when you get serious about asking questions all the time. One interesting question seems to fire brain activity that may appear to be random but with close scrutiny is connected. My experience has been that the effort to find the connection brings little insight, so I've learned to ignore the leap and focus on the seemingly new topic. I suggest you do the same.)

I can remember only one time in my corporate career when my employer asked what I knew about our competition. As it happened, I knew quite a lot about a new product that was being introduced by one of our hottest competitors because one of my customers had just gotten a bid from them and had given me a copy. I had read and filed the information. I'm ashamed to admit that it had never occurred to me that this might be important information for the whole organization, and if I hadn't been asked, it would have remained buried in my file.

Employees are consumers before they are employees, and many of them choose to do business with the organizations that vie for the attention and the dollars of your customers. Or they know people who regularly interact with your competition. How are you mining the information they have?

Even more interesting, there is the possibility that your employees may have some insight that you don't into who the competition really is. I remember attending an American Booksellers Association BookExpo in 1995 without hearing one bookstore owner mention Amazon.com. I have to believe that many of them had heard about the new company, but most seemed to dismiss it as a fad for the few. They were focusing on the growth of the large bookstore chains, a serious threat to be sure, but nothing compared to the impact of Internet book buying.

I'm pretty confident that out there somewhere is an Amazon.com-like competitor for at least part of your business. Asking this question might just give you the heads-up you need.

■ ▓ ■

▮ ▮ ▮ ▮ ▮ ▮ ▮ ▮ ▮ WHAT DID YOU LEARN? ▮ ▮ ▮ ▮ ▮ ▮ ▮ ▮ ▮ ▮

It is a dangerous thing to assume what people know. Did that thought cross your mind as you asked these questions? I've known young business people with MBAs from top business schools, who lacked what I considered to be a basic understanding of how their organization worked. Leaders ask the questions in this chapter, not to find out how much people don't know, but to discover where they need to focus their teaching.

Asking these questions and getting less than stellar answers isn't cause for depression, despair, and another cup of coffee with a colleague drunk to the ain't-it-awful-what-these-kids-don't-know refrain. Leaders take the answers to these questions as an energizing start-

> It is a healthy thing now and then to hang a question mark on the things you have long taken for granted.
>
> —Bertrand Russell, English mathematician and philosopher

ing point for action. They are excited to develop a plan for their team to get smarter about their work. They work their plan and ask the questions again as a way to chart their plan's success. They make sure each new member of their team is brought into the organization with the knowledge and tools necessary for them to be a full participant right from the beginning.

How about you? Think these questions might work in your world? You'll never know till you ask.

▪ ▪ ▪ ▪ ▪ ▪ ▪ ▪ ▪ ▪ **CHAPTER THREE WORKSHEET** ▪ ▪ ▪ ▪ ▪ ▪ ▪ ▪ ▪ ▪

1. What question in Chapter 3 did you find most challenging? Why?

_____

_____

_____

_____

_____

_____

_____

2. What other questions about the business did they make you think of?

_____

_____

_____

_____

_____

_____

_____

3. What basic business issues does your team need to learn about?

_____

_____

_____

_____

_____

_____

_____

4. What is your plan for making sure that they learn these things?

_____

_____

_____

_____

_____

_____

5. What one thing do you most want to remember from this chapter?

_____

_____

_____

_____

_____

_____

OTHER NOTES

_____

_____

_____

_____

_____

chapter 4

deeper questions leaders need to ask employees

BEFORE YOU rush out and start asking more questions, there are a few things to keep in mind. Asking questions takes time. Asking questions implies that you're going to listen to the answers. Asking these kinds of questions will annoy some people. Understanding each of these issues will help you formulate your questioning strategy, so let's take a look at each.

▌ Asking questions takes time. Don't kid yourself about this one. You can't approach people with important questions without allowing for the time it takes to hear the answers. When faced with a good question, most people actually think for a while, formulate their answer, deliver it, and expect a response. Often the response is a follow-up question that starts the process all over again. This takes time. It is rude to ask a question if you don't have the time to listen to and absorb the answer. It is inconsiderate to interrupt someone's day and ask them a question without determining if they have the time to answer.

Many leaders don't ask questions because of the time factors involved. When things settle down, they say, then I'll have the time to ask questions. If you are a leader who's waiting for things to settle down, you're going to be waiting a long time. You need to make the time to ask questions. It's your job.

Asking questions implies that you're going to listen to the answers. Remember the story about the man who wanted a note to his wife to prove that he'd passed my listening course? Remember my answer? Understanding the process of good listening doesn't ensure actually applying those principles.

Have you ever had a conversation with a person who kept looking at their watch while you're speaking? Most of us use the time while another person is speaking to develop our responses to their words (or what we think they'll say since we're not really listening anyway). That's not listening. Asking a question and listening to the answer involves staying engaged in the answer from beginning to end. No matter how long it takes the answerer to get to the end.

Asking questions and then practicing poor listening skills is a very bad idea. If you're not willing to sharpen your listening skills, you'd be better off not asking questions at all.

Asking these questions will annoy some people. Not everyone will be thrilled with your newfound enthusiasm for asking questions that go beyond the generally expected business questions. Expect some rolling of the eyes, double takes, and downright avoidance behavior. Just don't let these behaviors

> **Asking the right question takes as much skill as giving the right answers.**
>
> —Robert Half, American personnel agency executive

stop you from asking. People are suspicious of leaders who start asking questions because they're confused by new behavior, because they fear the reprisal for an honestly answered tough question, or because they're just plain cynical.

Don't let reluctance on the part of others influence your commitment to asking these questions. Acknowledge their existence, explain your intentions again, and keep asking.

Don't run out and bombard people with questions. Pick the right question for the right person at the right time. Learning how to ask questions is about strategic thinking.

The time you spend thinking strategically about the questions you ask will be time well-spent and the answers you get will be of greater value.

One more word of advice. If you're having trouble deciding what question to start with in order to go deeper with this behavior, why not try this one: *What would you think of a leader who is known for the quality questions they ask?* The answers just might provide the motivation you need to keep asking.

■ ■ ■

20. What gets in the way of your doing your job?

For years we have all joked and/or raged about the "it's not my job" attitudes we've encountered in organizations, big and small. Have you ever stopped to ask yourself if there is a customer somewhere who thought that way about your organization? Or have you honestly wondered if you've got employees that are looking for jobs elsewhere because they believe that no one in your organization cares enough to fix internal systems? Dr. W. Edward Deming, the man whose name is forever linked with quality, believed that 85 percent of quality problems in the workplace are caused by systems, not by an individual's inefficiencies. Our organizations are filled with policies and procedures that prohibit people from doing their best to satisfy our customers, and you need to know where it's happening in yours.

This is the first risky-to-answer question we've encountered in our list. The answer to this particular question can often be a department or a person's name. Please remember that an answerer may need some time to decide whether or not it is actually safe to tell you the truth. Describing an outdated policy or explaining an easy-to-streamline procedure is a fairly safe answer. Identifying a bottleneck department or an obstructionist co-worker is another decision process entirely. You will have to consider time and place when you venture forth with this question. A comfortable pause after asking a high-risk question will facilitate your receiving a thoughtful and productive answer.

A word of caution: One of the ground rules of good questioning is that when a question is asked and an answer is given, the questioner does not (and often should not) respond. Given an answer, you should simply acknowledge the information, clarify any ambiguities, and assure the answerer that their opinion is valuable and will be considered. If you express an opinion or make a promise based on a single response to your question, you might find yourself in the middle of something more complex than that one answer indicated. This is especially problematic when a response to your question points a finger at an individual. An emotional reaction from you may satisfy the answerer but cause great difficulty for the other person mentioned. Your best response to this situation is "Thank you for bringing this to my attention. As I understand it, your situation is [restate the problem]. You have my word that I will look into this matter and will get back to you with a resolution. Please know that I appreciate your efforts to make our organization better." Now your job becomes one of detective. By asking more questions and listening to the additional answers carefully, you'll be able to fulfill your promise to deliver a resolution to the original answerer. It may not be exactly what they wanted or envisioned, but they will appreciate the fact that you kept your word and followed through.

■ ■ ■

21. What does our leadership team do that gets in the way of your doing your job?

One of the most often identified roles of a leader is that of barrier buster. Leaders get into trouble when they fall into a pattern of doing the jobs of the people who report to them rather than creating an environment that allows the right people to do the right things. Successful leaders are eager to help their people find ways to be productive by coaching them appropriately. They let their teams know that if they encounter a barrier that is beyond their ability to tackle, the leader expects that the team will ask for help. That is the moment when leaders need to roll up their sleeves and get to work on behalf of the team.

But what happens when the leadership team is the barrier? Asking *What does our leadership team do that gets in the way of you doing your job?* requires persistence and courage.

Persistence because the first time you ask this question, you are most likely to be answered with a quick "nothing" or "they're doing okay" response. Don't miss the internal dialogue that will undoubtedly be running through the answerer's mind. "What kind of a fool does this person take me for? Like I'm going to answer this question!" And honestly, can you blame them for thinking that? So, ask the question, but don't expect quality answers the first time around. The more you ask other questions and handle the answers appropriately, the more likely it is that when you ask this question again, you will get more truthful answers.

Courage because the responses you get might be painful to hear. It has been my experience while working with leaders that the farther up you are in the hierarchy, the less likely you are to receive an accurate picture of the organization's day-to-day workings.

Unless, of course, you've been asking questions long enough to be trusted. You may hear things about your team's behavior and maybe even about your own behavior that will require some soul-searching and change on your part. Don't ask this question if you're not ready to hear and act on the answers. By the way, if you're not ready to act—get ready fast!

22. What's a recent management decision you didn't understand?

Your goal in asking this question is to determine if you need to work on the quality of the decisions you make or the way you communicate your decisions. These are two different things. You need to determine if people don't understand *why* a decision was made or find out if the *way* you delivered your decision was flawed. A review of the emotional reactions that decisions often evoke is seldom made before the decision is delivered.

Let's deal with the emotions first. Employee survey after employee survey reports that one of the greatest motivators in the workplace is the connected feeling employees get when they understand what's going on in their organization. If you need convincing, walk through a workplace after a news item that reveals a change in their organization appears in the media. Nothing makes people feel more like pawns in a grand chess game than being blindsided by company information from a source outside the organization. Trust me, no matter how logical the decision might have been or how practical the change is, when a decision or a change is announced in this fashion, people react badly, and the organization suffers. Hearing things from the newspaper is an extreme example, but many big decisions are delivered to employees without a well-thought-out internal communication plan, and most day-to-day decisions are delivered without any explanations at all. Underestimating the emotional reaction to a decision, based on its mode of delivery, is risky business.

How about the content of the decision? When leaders take the time to do a good job explaining their decisions, they have accepted the critical leader role of educator. No one in their right mind would empower a young teenager to jump into a car and drive alone before they were properly trained, had plenty of practice, and had passed the test. Yet very few of the organizations that preach empowerment take the necessary steps to make sure their people have a broad understanding of how their organization works, establish levels of learning that correspond to levels of decision-making authority, and deliver a constant stream of usable feedback for all employees. A leader who helps people understand the process behind a decision is educating them for the time when they will have to make decisions on their own.

■ ■ ■

23. How could we communicate management decisions more effectively?

I can't remember exactly where I heard it for the first time, but I do remember the general circumstances. There was a group of us seated around a table. Flipcharts covered the walls, and markers and half-used Post-it notepads littered the table. Our work had progressed nicely up until the last agenda item. Our task was to agree on a way to disseminate information on a recent decision. The conversation seemed to go around in circles. Someone took a deep breath, made eye contact with each of us and said, "Do you think it's likely that we can develop any sort of communication plan by continuing to pool our ignorance about how this decision was made?" What a wonderful question. That's exactly what we were doing, talking about something we had no real information about or insight into, and yet it took a courageous questioner to point us in the right direction. We adjourned the meeting and went out to do our homework. We couldn't talk about a decision until we understood it. Asking *How could we communicate management decisions more effectively?* can save you from expending effort based on ignorance.

Wanting to provide helpful context for a management decision isn't enough. You have to discover what communication format will send your message most effectively. Communication based on a one-size-fits-all philosophy is wrong more often than it is right. Communication delivered one time, in one way, will never satisfy people's needs to understand. Asking this question will help you determine an effective communication strategy. Asking it over time and monitoring the changing answers will help you (and others in your organization) formulate communication strategies that really add value. Remember, from the customer's perspective, an interaction with an employee is the basis upon which they judge the organization. Doesn't it make sense to be sure that all employees—from janitors to senior vice presidents—know and understand what's going on?

By the way, there is no excuse for not getting your internal communications right. In this day of instant, easy, and inexpensive communications technology, those organizations that don't do a great job communicating with their teams and employees are, I would bet, experiencing higher than industry average turnover, lower than average morale, and increasing customer complaints. This might be a good time to review how creatively you're using the communications technology you have and to develop some new strategies to get your key messages and decisions from one end of the organization to the other.

■　■　■

24. If you could change one thing about our organization's collective behavior, what would it be?

Many organizations develop a list of values—conduct they uphold as their guide for the behavior of all employees. These values are often published and distributed. Too often, these values are thought to be real just because they've been put on paper, but they become fiction in practice. Values are too important to exist only on paper— they need to live in an organization's daily activities.

The challenge successful leaders should give themselves is to use their values as a measurement and evaluation tool. Leaders need to praise and encourage the good behaviors, monitor the difference between actual and desired behaviors, and correct bad behaviors before they become institutionalized. The challenge for most leaders is to maintain an accurate picture of the real state of their workplace. This question can help you do just that. When leaders

> **Advice is what we ask for when we already know the answer but wish we didn't.**
>
> —Erica Jong, American writer

understand that organizations, like people, have both good and bad habits, there is potential for positive change. Finding the gaps between what gets said and what gets done gives you a place to start.

Think about what you would (and have) done when confronted with situations where your stated values have been contradicted. If you say you have respect for people in your values statement, would you fire your top salesperson because they repeatedly berated the clerical staff? If you value creativity, would you decline a job because you couldn't see any way of adding innovation to the client's existing processes? If, according to your mission statement, customers come first, would you withhold a bonus for the vice president of customer service when your customer service targets were missed? What about your own bonus? Do you practice what you preach?

Believe me, if you don't live your stated values, there will be gaps between the behavior you want your organization to practice and the behavior I'd observe if I spent time with your people. Finding those gaps should be your priority, unless, of course, you want to revise that value list you so proudly print in your annual report.

This question begs for a follow-up. Try this one—*How can we get our behavior back on track?*—and listen well.

■ ■ ■

25. What's a potential benefit we could offer that would be helpful to you?

This question is very specific, and it might not apply to you, but if you have any input on employee benefits or if you have responsibility for benefit recommendations or decisions, ask away.

Over the years I've noticed a small, common behavior between partners in successful and happy long-term relationships. When a holiday or birthday approaches, they have a conversation that starts something like this: "What's on your list this year?" I wish I could convey the warm tone of voice that's behind this simple sentence. Don't allow yourself to read it with disinterest or sarcasm because that's not the way it is said by these partners. Don't jump to the conclusion that it's said at every gift opportunity either. These partners haven't abandoned the notion of a surprise, but they have come to realize that gifts that are grounded in real needs are better investments.

What does this have to do with employee benefits? A lot. Years ago our workplaces were filled with a fairly homogeneous group of people. Deciding on a new benefit was fairly easy. But, in case you haven't looked recently, things have changed. In one department you probably have a Baby Boomer looking at retirement issues, an older GenX with young children, a younger GenX looking for opportunities to learn and develop new skills either with you or someone else, and a GenY starting their working life. Your employees are increasingly diverse—different races, ethnic backgrounds, and life experiences. The Vietnam War and protests, the assassination of JFK, and mornings with Captain Kangaroo are seminal events and icons for some and ancient history for others. Desert Storm, the Challenger explosion, and MTV hold the same positions for others. One size does not fit all in this group; in truth, one size doesn't even fit most!

As you work to provide benefits for your employees while being a good steward of your organization's resources, you need specific information about the people in your organization. Benefit programs that don't meet the varied needs of your employees are a waste and reflect poor leadership. Asking this question won't make these decisions easy, but it will make you a better decision-maker.

■ ■ ■

26. What is it like to work on a team in our organization?

If anyone is taking a vote on the most misused business word, let me know. I want to place a vote. The word *team* is often used to describe any group of people working on a task. *Team*, however, actually means something very specific. A team is a collection of people with a shared, meaningful purpose and an emotional connection who work together toward a common goal. This isn't the place to debate the definition or the value of teams, but this is the place to consider the importance of asking *What is it like to work on a team in our organization?* if you do consider your organization to be team-based.

The answers to this question will be greatly dependent on the team's current situation. Teams, like individuals, departments, and organizations, have good days and bad days, and the answer to this question will be influenced by which kind of day it is. After listening to a litany of problems or a joyful description of successes, you'll need to probe further. Your intent in asking this question is to uncover the totality of a team's experience in your organization.

If people mention a lack of support, scarcity of resources, insufficient recognition, or endless meetings that seem to be a waste of time, pay attention. Teams don't just happen. You can't expect that by putting a group of smart people into a room together and calling them a team, they'll become one. Teams need to be nurtured, and that's the job of a leader. Based on the answers you get to this question, it might be time to review how you form, train, and launch your teams. Maybe you need to review the charters of your existing teams. How about planning some project reviews that not only look at a team's progress toward their goals but that also include a review of how effectively the team is working together.

Somewhere, in a positive answer to this question, people might talk eagerly about the opportunities they've had to learn new things, develop new skills, and nurture new relationships. When you get these kinds of responses, you've learned that the team experience in your organization is shaping up to both the member's and the organization's benefit.

■ ■ ■

27. How do you feel at the start of your workweek?

This question marks a change in the focus of our inquiries. Until now the questions have asked people to share the facts and information they know. Fact and information answers are important—in fact, business runs on them. But they don't tell the whole story. Organizations are filled with people, and people are filled with feelings. Leaders who believe that they can focus their work on the tasks at hand and leave the "soft stuff" to the human resources department shouldn't really call themselves leaders! If you choose to continue to accept my challenge and focus your attention on the way people feel about working in your organization, the next several questions are the perfect place to start. Remember, the process is simple—ask, listen, and say thanks. Take the risk. I know you can do it.

Remember those questions on intelligence tests that give you a list of words and then ask which word doesn't belong? Try this one: Enthusiasm, Passion, Excitement, Fun, Work. What is your answer? Hopefully, you came to the conclusion that this was an example of a poorly constructed or trick question. They all go together, don't they?

Or, maybe you're wearing your Dilbert hat and wonder why anyone would bother to ask such an obvious question. Work has nothing to do with those other words. If that's your response, shame on you! Think of the energy an organization would have if everyone in it agreed that enthusiasm, passion, excitement, fun, and work were synonyms. What could your organization accomplish if just half your employees believed that? Has it occurred to you that even 15 percent would be an improvement? Are you clueless about how people feel when they enter your doors? Believe me, how your employees feel as they start their workweek provides great insight about how they'll interact with each other and with your customers.

When you decide to start talking about the feelings that fill your workplace, make a commitment to find, support, and showcase the positive ones. Don't read that to mean you should ignore or dismiss the negative emotions; just don't make them the center of your action. Look for ways to increase enthusiasm for solving problems, ignite passion for learning, encourage excitement around success, foster fun as a stress reliever, and discourage seeing work as a four-letter word. You'll be doing your job.

28. How do you feel at the end of your workweek?

Watching people as they enter the workplace at the beginning of the workweek gives you one view of organizational morale. Watching them as they leave at the end of the week gives you a different perspective. That's why both questions are included as significant questions to ask.

What you're really asking with this question is *What does our work environment do to your spirit?* This is a question asked by brave leaders. The answer you're looking for goes something like this. "Let me think. At the end of the week I'm exhausted and exhilarated. Some weeks it's more one than the other, but it's always a combination of both." Exhaustion means that a person has given their all when they do their work. Exhilaration means that they believe that their work has meaning and that they have derived satisfaction from doing it.

The answers you're apt to get when you ask this question might be very different from the one I outlined. In fact, the answer you get to this question might be an uneasy giggle followed by silence, a confused look with a mumbled "Why do you care," or a blunt "It's none of your business." Those answers tell you a lot, too. Leaders ignore the spirit in their workplace at their own peril. Don't ask this question unless you intend to take action to change the status quo.

Before you turn the page, allow me to ask you a quick question: *How do you feel at the end of your workweek?* Do the words "exhausted" and "exhilarated" play a part in your answer?

29. What volunteer work do you do?

At one time in my life, I worked for a temporary agency. One of the assignments they sent me to was at a large manufacturing plant where my job consisted of answering the phone for a department. (Just a quick aside. Why would an organization put a temporary employee in a front-line, customer contact position? I cringe when I remember how many times I said I was sorry because I had no idea how to answer a customer's question. I was sorry until I realized that I seemed to be the only one who cared.)

During the week I worked there, I overheard the leaders of the department talking about the lack of creativity their people exhibited. Later the same day, I observed the team working out a creative solution to a major problem facing their company bowling team. I've thought about that contradiction a lot since then. I've learned

> I also have learned that when we begin listening to each other, and when we talk about things that matter to us, the world begins to change
>
> —Margaret J. Wheatley,
> American scientist and writer

that the leaders were right in one way. In an environment that doesn't expect people to be creative, they won't be creative. However, those same people will be creative in an environment that challenges them to be creative. I've also learned that those leaders could have had a creative workforce if they had asked, *What volunteer work do you do?*

People volunteer for causes they believe in and for jobs in which they can put their skills to good use. Think about what you'd learn about the hidden talents in your organization by asking this question. You may be surprised by the people you discover. An accountant that coaches a winning soccer team. An administrative assistant who teaches watercolor painting at the local community college. A customer service representative who leads a fund-raising campaign. "So what?" you may ask. So what indeed. Look at the hidden talents you didn't know about or, more importantly, didn't expect. This is a question that requires listening to the answer without reaction. You may hear some responses that challenge strongly held beliefs, and it is human nature to let that incredulity show on your face. Keep in mind that a look that expresses surprise or curiosity is okay. Incredulity is an insult.

Many of the specifics you learn when asking this question won't have practical application—unless, of course, you'd like your administrative assistant to illustrate your monthly reports. But these answers will force you to look at the people you work with through new eyes, seeing different possibilities, and changing some limiting expectations. This kind of challenge is good for a leader.

30. What makes you proud of working as a part of our organization?

The company knew they had to do something. Customer satisfaction ratings were dropping, employee turnover was rising, and nobody wanted to talk about morale. Serious competition was looming. A group of leaders were appointed to do something about the situation and to do it fast. Meeting after meeting produced idea after idea. Consultants were hired, and a final decision was reached. "We'll create a video that tells everyone why they should be happy that they work here," they decided. "We'll prove that the future's bright by showing our grandly produced video to everyone. Spare no expense," they said. "Just get it done."

So, the script was written, the actors were hired, and the locations scouted. Production began and money was spent. The final version was shown to the executive team and they beamed at each other. This would do it; things would change now. After all, they had spared no expense.

Employees were ushered into the meeting room and given plastic cups filled with sparkling grape juice. The lights dimmed and the video began. The music was powerful and the videography impressive. The leaders sitting in the front of the room led the applause and raised their glasses in a toast to the renewed commitment they were certain everyone in attendance felt. People filed out of the room talking about their weekend plans. That's when I heard one of the participants say, "I can't believe they're trying to get us to put our hats back on with that crap!"

No one else seemed to hear his comment. Curious, I followed him out of the building and asked, "What hat?"

"Oh," he replied offhandedly, "When I first started, fifteen years ago, we all had hats with the company's name and logo. I was like most guys; we wore them all the time. We wanted everyone to know where we worked. We were proud to work here. I haven't worn my hat for a long time."

Many organizations, in an attempt to improve morale, spend dollars, time, and energy externally and forget that morale is an inside job. Please don't ask consultants to help you improve morale in your organization. Start by asking this question yourself of the people on your team, really listen to the answers, and go to work.

■ ■ ■

31. What's something you've learned in the past week?

Here's a thought. School's never out for the professional. How does that make you feel? Excited or depressed? Continuous formal learning, whether in the university classroom or the corporate training room, is a necessity—not a luxury—for all of us. But there is another, informal style of learning that leaders need to encourage. It is learning because of curiosity and need.

I was at a speaker showcase several years ago when I heard a presenter by the name of Bob Prichard say, "When you're not learning—someone somewhere else is. When you meet—guess who has the advantage." I've carried that concept with me every day since. As a leader, you need to ask yourself if you could honestly say that your team is smarter today than they were a year ago. If they are, do you know how they got that way? Good business means, in part, replicating effective behavior, but you can't replicate behavior that you don't know about. Start asking questions about learning.

Finding out how your people learn can be a fascinating exercise. You'll find those who learn by doing, some who learn by listening, and others who need to see a picture (either real or imagined) before something sinks in. The advantage of a supported do-it-yourself learning environment is that everyone can have their learning the way they need it. You can be part of the support process. Does your organization have a library? Does it have both books and books on tape? Are there whiteboards and flipcharts available for everyone's use? Do you understand that doodling, muttering under your breath, and standing up during a meeting can all be signs of a person learning? It appears as though there could be a lot for you to learn.

Why bother? Because of the competition. You can bet they're learning, and if they are and you aren't, the future starts looking dim. So, start asking a few questions. Who knows, you might learn something!

∎ ∎ ∎

32. What brings you joy in your work?

Some people live their lives as though joy were a very limited resource. As if they were allocated an amount at birth, squandered much of their share during childhood and must now, as responsible adults, hoard their remaining supply for some unspecified time in the future. Given these parameters, why would anyone in their right mind waste joy on work?

Let me think. Artists often do. Teachers do, I hope. The waiter at my favorite Wausau restaurant, The Back When Café, does. The vendors I do repeat business with do. The most successful leaders I've known do. The organizations that thrive, year in and year out, do. If you agree with the conventional wisdom that joy is an endangered species, then these people are fools. The day will come when they'll simply run out of their allotment of joy—and won't you have the last laugh then. However, what if they're wrong? What if you run out of life with your allotment of joy untouched?

Work is a great place to express joy. If you look, you'll see that there are so many little opportunities for happiness when you work with people you respect, do tasks that make a difference, and use the talents you've been given. If you read that and don't agree that your job affords those possibilities, then you're either in the wrong job or not paying attention. No matter which is true, you can and should make some changes.

Remember these thoughts as you listen to the answers to this question. Do people find joy in their work at your organization? What are the implications for you if they don't? You can help people find joy in their work by showing them how what they do matters. Many people in today's workplace have no idea how the things they do on a daily basis affect the success or failure of their organization. A receptionist needs to understand that the way he answers a phone could make or break the biggest deal your organization may ever have. A filing clerk needs to know that her daily efforts make it possible for the customer service team to respond quickly to a customer request. A pipe fitter deserves to look at the architect's drawing and know that, because of her efforts, the building she's working on will shelter the children at a daycare center. It is your job to help all team members understand the importance of their work. Do that and watch the joy spread.

■ ■ ■

33. What do you do just for the fun of it?

This is a great question for people who find it hard to listen. Your assignment when you ask this question is to watch even more than you listen. Watch people's faces light up, their bodies relax, and their voices resonate with energy. Don't stop listening to what they're saying, but pay special attention to the transformation. The answers will be as varied as the people who give them, but the physical changes will be similar. There is a physical response when people talk about or do something that brings them glee.

That's why laughter is important in the workplace. Hey, stress is a part of our work life that isn't going to go away. Hard work, repetitive tasks, and frightening situations all cause stress in the workplace. But not all stress is bad. The things we do for fun are often hard work (ever try to dig out a garden?), repetitive (ever quilt a bedspread?), or scary (bungee jumping, anyone?). But we have fun doing those activities. Understanding that what feels like fun for one person can cause negative stress in another is a valuable lesson. Leaders who learn about the fun profiles of their people can use that information creatively when handing out assignments. You might have people whose eyes sparkle when they talk about their latest work endeavor.

There's a bonus for listening to the answers to this question. You'll be amazed at the hidden skills you'll uncover. There will be stories of confident leadership, technical ingenuity, and amazing creativity. You'll discover writers, salespeople, and inventors in your midst. One leader I know, after being overwhelmed by the answers he received from asking this question, arranged a special interest fair over a lunch hour. Based on the response to displays people created and the conversations that occurred during the exhibits, the company dedicated a room and developed a series of How To... classes organized and run by a volunteer committee. Their people now come in early and stay late to learn a language, paint a picture, and master spreadsheet development for kid's sports teams. It's a fun place to work.

34. What gives your life meaning?

This is a dangerous question to ask and if you haven't established a reputation as a careful listener, a credible confidant, and a thoughtful leader, don't ask it. If you do ask it without these credentials, you will be perceived as nosey, intrusive, and even phony.

Walk into your favorite bookstore or log on to Amazon.com and look for books about meaning and purpose in your life and work. You'll find lots of them. Even if you can't bring yourself to leave the business books, you'll find chapters on purpose and meaning in almost all those books too. Finding meaning in life is important.

Before you run around dropping this question on others, you need to answer it for yourself. It's okay if you can't answer this question when you ask it for the first time of others, so long as you are willing to share your ongoing quest for your own answer. This question is actually more about the process then an answer. Some people find their purpose early in life, some grow into an understanding, and others need many years and experiences to reach an *Aha!* It is the people who never ask themselves the question who miss out.

Find Viktor Frankel's book *Man's Search for Meaning*, read it, and give copies away. Ponder Socrates' words, "The unexamined life is not worth living," and have it printed on cards that you can give to others. Listen to what others say (and don't say) when you ask this question, and be willing to ask it of yourself.

■ ■ ■

■ ■ ■ ■ ■ ■ ■ ■ ■ **WHAT DID YOU LEARN?** ■ ■ ■ ■ ■ ■ ■ ■ ■

Okay, you've asked a lot of varied questions. Now what? Well, first, ask yourself what you learned—about yourself.

What did it feel like asking all these questions? Was it uncomfortable at first and easier as you practiced? Maybe you discovered that you got impatient having to listen as people went on and on with their answers. Perhaps you're not as good a listener as you thought you were. You might have found yourself eagerly listening to something you never dreamed could capture your interest. I hope you found that people became more eager to talk to you and that your reputation as a leader grew—not because you had all the answers, but because you asked the very best questions.

What did you learn about the people in your organization? How different are they and how much do they have in common? How often were you surprised by something you didn't know about their

> **That is the essence of science: Ask an impertinent question, and you are on the way to a pertinent answer.**
>
> —Jacob Bronowski,
> Polish mathematician

work, their concerns, and their caring? I hope you have a better understanding about the responsibilities of a leader. Of course, you need to make sure the work gets done and your customers are satisfied, but your job is more than that. The bottom line for a leader covers it all, finances and fears, productivity and passion, shareholder value and living your values.

What are you going to do with the answers? Is it time for an action plan, a leadership team retreat, or an all-employee meeting? Do you need to revisit your mission, vision, and value statements? Revamp your training programs? Or reconfigure your offices? You're the only one who can figure it out, but you know what you need to do. So, start doing it. And while you're at it, keep asking questions. You'll be a better leader for it!

⦀ ⦀ ⦀ ⦀ ⦀ ⦀ ⦀ ⦀ ⦀ **CHAPTER FOUR WORKSHEET** ⦀ ⦀ ⦀ ⦀ ⦀ ⦀ ⦀ ⦀ ⦀

1. Which of the questions in this chapter did you find most challenging? Why?

_____

_____

_____

_____

_____

_____

_____

_____

2. What other questions did this chapter make you think of?

_____

_____

_____

_____

_____

_____

_____

3. How do you feel about asking more personal questions of the people who work for you? Why?

_____

_____

_____

_____

_____

_____

_____

4. How did your people react to your asking these kinds of questions?

_____

_____

_____

_____

_____

_____

5. Why do you think they had that reaction?

_____

_____

_____

_____

_____

_____

_____

_____

6. What is the one thing you want to remember most from this chapter?

_____

_____

_____

_____

_____

_____

_____

OTHER NOTES

_____

_____

_____

_____

_____

_____

questions to ask in special situations

LEADERS RARELY get days filled with business as usual. A leader's day often consists of a string of unique situations that they are expected to handle. What better way to prepare for these special situations than to think about the questions you might want to have ready when any of these common leadership interactions happen? I've defined four Special Situations when having questions at the ready will be a real benefit.

1. QUESTIONS FOR NEW EMPLOYEES. One of the best parts of a leader's job is to welcome new employees to their team. My assumption is that your organization has a formal orientation program for your new hires. (If it doesn't, you're the one who brings up the need for such a session at every opportunity, aren't you?) The questions in this section are about the time you personally devote to welcoming someone new to your team. Nothing will have a

> **It is better to debate a question without settling it than to settle a question without debating it.**
>
> —Joseph Joubert,
> French essayist and moralist

greater impact on a new hire than that first, personal interaction with their new boss. Use the questions in this section as a way to start an interesting dialogue with the new members of your team.

2. QUESTIONS FOR COACHING AND MENTORING SESSIONS. In most organizations, leaders participate in some form of coaching and mentoring sessions for the people on their team and possibly for people on other teams. These programs can range from formal systems to informal, spontaneous hallway conversations. Leaders are assigned or sought out. Leaders who take this role seriously (my bias is that if you call yourself a leader, you do) will find the questions in this section helpful.

3. QUESTIONS FOR NEWLY PROMOTED LEADERS. One of your key responsibilities as a leader will be to identify, nurture, and mentor new leaders. Moving someone into a place where they can be considered and promoted to leadership positions can be a source of great pride. The questions in this section will help your new leaders build their confidence and see their roles as leaders from a fresh perspective. Taking the time to ask these questions will be a meaningful investment in the future of your organization.

4. **QUESTIONS DURING A CRISIS.** It would be nice to believe that you could be a leader and never have to deal with a serious crisis. Nice to believe, but probably unrealistic. Thinking about your responsibilities before a crisis is infinitely better than trying to determine them during the crisis. The questions in this section will help you if and when a crisis hits your team or organization.

Your willingness to take the time and find the places to use the questions in this chapter says a lot about your personal commitment to leadership. Other questions in this book may stretch your courage when you ask them, may be just plain tough to ask, or may challenge the status quo of your organization. The questions in this chapter will be helpful to ask and need to be part of your stock-in-trade.

■ ■ ■

QUESTIONS FOR NEW EMPLOYEES

35. Why did you decide to join our firm...really?

Remember the last time you took a new job with a new employer? The reasons that brought you to that decision were undoubtedly many and complex. Did anyone ever ask you why? Probably not. Why don't you do something different and start asking new hires why they decided to join your company?

Asking this question will provide you with insights on several levels. You'll learn about your organization's reputation in the industry. You might gain insight into your organization's relative position on salaries and benefits. You might learn something about your reputation as a leader. You'll gain insight into your new hire's decision-making process. You can gauge their reaction when asked an unexpected question. Lots of good information, don't you think?

This is a great place to reiterate the value of silence when asking a challenging question. Years ago, when I was in sales, I learned a valuable technique. It was presented as a sales technique, but I've learned that it works in many different situations for many different people including salespeople, customer service representatives, spouses, parents, and leaders, to name a few. It's deceptively simple, as many effective techniques are, and it works like this. When you ask a question, shut up until the answerer answers.

Sounds pretty straightforward, doesn't it? Try it, and you'll discover how difficult it is to execute. Most of us are uncomfortable with silence, and so we jump in to fill it. This behavior has lots of consequences—different ones in different situations—but all of them serious. In the sales world, the commonly held wisdom says it this way: The first person who talks after the question loses. When a questioner fills the silence after their own question, they do lose, big-time.

This is a perfect question to use to practice and develop your comfort with silence. It's the *really* at the end of the question that guarantees the need for the answerer to pause to consider their reply. The addition of that simple word pushes the answerer beyond the quick, glib response they might have had ready after considering how much truth you're looking for.

So, ask this question and wait, comfortably, while maintaining eye contact, and then wait some more. You'll continue to be surprised how critical silence is for getting good answers to questions, and this question will give you lots of opportunity to practice.

■ ■ ■

36. If you had to describe our organization in one word, what would that word be?

More words adding up to longer answers do not necessarily provide more insight. Sometimes questions that force brevity can provide interesting answers that are easy to compare. This question falls into that category.

Imagine asking this question of all new hires for six months. Depending on the size of your organization and your rates of turnover and expansion, you could develop and keep track of the one-word answers pretty easily. What would be the value of that? I can think of three.

1. As your list of descriptive words grows, you can compare them and look for consistency of expectations from those who join your organization or department. What do you think it means if half the people respond with words like "fun," "energetic," and "creative," and the other half of the people you've asked respond with words like "stable," "traditional," and "respectable"? My analysis of those responses would be that half of the people who responded were going to be disappointed. It's up to you to decide which half. A split response like this tells you that you haven't established a consistent image in your marketplace. A consistent response that you like tells you your image is intact. A consistent response you don't like means you have some actions to take.

2. As your list of words grows, you'll gain insight into the way people feel about your organization or department. Leaders have responsibilities for feelings as well as facts, and you

might as well find out how people are feeling as they join your team. Waiting until later isn't exactly stellar leadership behavior.

3. Keep track of whom you've asked, how they answered, and when you asked them. Use a milestone—four- to six-month anniversaries would work—and ask the question again: *Now that you've been with us for a while, what one word would you use to describe our organization?* Asking and comparing these answers will give you insight into the consistency of experience your people have as they become part of your team.

Don't let the fact that my imagination was limited to three possibilities stunt your thought processes. What are other ways you could use this information? Think about it.

37. What's a great question I could ask someone who's new to our organization?

This question is probably the most blatantly selfish question in the entire book. Finding good questions becomes an obsession for leaders who learn the value and power of asking questions. What better way to find questions than to ask for them?

Asking for questions within your organization works for a while. Every leader, even those who don't make questioning a priority, will have a few questions they routinely ask. But you'll often find that within an organization, questions seem to cluster around certain themes. Asking for new questions from people who come from different organizational backgrounds will provide you with a whole new set of possible questions.

But there is another, less selfish reason for asking this question of a new hire. Their reaction will provide you with insights into their comfort with a leader who asks questions. Some people will eagerly share questions, some will haltingly respond with a question, and others will stare blankly as if you've asked the most bizarre question ever uttered.

The eager sharer is telling you either that they've joined your team from a question-rich culture or that they understand the power of questions and are happy to share. Work with this new employee to strengthen their commitment to questioning and to encourage them to share new questions as they find them.

The slow responder is letting you know that they haven't had a lot of experience with leaders who ask questions but are willing to participate. Make sure you thank them for their contribution and encourage them to make others in the future. Keep them in mind for some gentle questioning in the near future so you can help them understand this part of your leadership style.

The blank looker is harder to read. They may be confused by a leader who asks questions, frightened by this level of interaction with their new leader, or genuinely surprised by the action of a leader asking them for their opinion. No matter which interpretation might be accurate, don't jump to a conclusion. It's now your job to find out which of these (or any of many other explanations) is the right one.

No matter which situation you encounter with this question, like asking any good question of the right person at the right time, you'll get valuable information that you'll be able to use in the future.

38. What questions can I answer for you?

If you don't ask this question shortly after you meet a new employee, if you don't keep silent long enough for them to respond, and if you don't answer truthfully any questions that they do ask, you've lost any chance for them to react positively to your questioning leadership style in the future. More than just providing information, this question is designed to begin the process of establishing trust.

Trust is a leader's stock-in-trade. Without trust, it is impossible to be a leader. You can be a manager, a boss, a dictator, or a ruler. You can order people to do things, require rules to be followed, inspire behavior from fear, or demand obedience, but you won't inspire confidence, encourage creativity, or be proud of yourself. You can't be a leader.

Trust is built and maintained through actions both big and small. Respectfully asking questions and taking appropriate actions based on the answers is one of the ways trust is built between leaders and followers. Demonstrating your willingness to really listen to all the

> **If a question can be put at all, then it can also be answered.**
>
> —Ludwig Wittgenstein,
> Austrian philosopher

people on your team or in your organization is another. Asking questions that go beyond the expected offers another path to trust.

Trust takes time to build, but it can be lost in a minute. As a leader who asks questions, you need to watch out for these trust-destroying behaviors:

▌ Asking a question without listening to the answers

▌ Expecting followers to take the time to answer your questions without taking the time to answer theirs

▌ Treating their questions or answers as trivial

▌ Missing an opportunity to ask the all-important follow-up question

▌ Not treating answers to questions with confidentiality (unless you've asked for permission to share an answer)

If you ever, because of an enormous brain cramp, come close to behaving in one of these ways, apologize at once, apologize repeatedly, apologize publicly (unless, of course, that would betray a confidence and dig the hole you're in even deeper), and then get to work rebuilding the trust you've lost.

Remember, even if the person involved accepts your first apology with a "Don't worry, it's not a big thing," don't believe him. Smile, nod, and do the trust-building work anyway.

▌ ▌ ▌

▌QUESTIONS FOR COACHING AND MENTORING SESSIONS

39. What are the strengths you bring to the workplace?

When you're in a coaching situation, I believe that this is the best beginning question. Not that it is easy for people to answer. Far from it. Many of us are filled with childhood admonitions like "Don't boast" and "Be humble." People who carry these messages often have great difficulty articulating their personal strengths. Some gave up trying years ago because the guilt they felt while giving themselves a personal pat on the back conflicted with the pride they were feeling. Wouldn't leading be easier if humans weren't so complex? But understanding our strengths is critical to success, and so it becomes a leader coach's job to help an individual compile this list of strengths.

Conventional wisdom suggests that leaders have the responsibility to search out, point out, and sometimes even (gasp!) beat out an employee's weaknesses. Once again, conventional wisdom seems to be wrong. Recent research by the Gallup Organization suggests that a leader who focuses attention on identifying and fostering the strengths of their employees will see improvement faster and further than those who focus on trying to improve weaknesses.

A list of strengths needs to be specific in order to be helpful. Coaches and mentors know how useless the "I'm good with people" response really is. So this question requires some automatic follow-up questions.

▌ What does being "good with people" mean to you?

▌ How do you do that?

▌ Can you give me an example of when you did that?

▌ What, of all the things you did in that situation, worked best?

▌ What kind of feedback did you get after that happened?

▌ How have you refined that skill over time?

All of these follow-up questions are designed to help your mentee understand their true strengths in real terms. After this kind of conversation, "I'm good with people" becomes "I know how to help two people in conflict find common ground and work together successfully." A much better answer to build on.

▌ ▌ ▌

40. What skills do you need to learn?

In the discussion of the last question, I suggested that building on strengths was a better way to go as a coach than trying to eliminate weaknesses. I hope I didn't leave you thinking that you never had to do anything with the latter. This is the question that moves you into the tricky arena of weaknesses.

No one likes to think (let alone talk) about their deficiencies—especially with their boss. Asking a person what they need to learn is something completely different. If you were to ask me this question, I'd give you answers that would include lifelong fantasies (watercolor painting), practical stretch goals (writing a novel), and an actual affects-my-job weakness (how to deliver tough feedback to a co-worker). Being about to put one of my well-known-to-me weaknesses in the middle of a list feels less dangerous than blurting out that I'm really bad at giving feedback. (Actually I'm bad at getting feedback, too, but I don't even admit that to myself. The beauty of the learning approach to weaknesses is that if I get to a class that addresses part of my developmental need, I'm likely to get practice on the other.)

A coaching or mentoring session that focuses on developing a practical learning plan for the immediate future will be far more fruitful in both the short and the long term for both of you.

41. What skills do you need to practice?

When coaches and mentors ask this question, they're taking responsibility in two areas—the quality of training programs and the quality of work experiences. Covers a lot of ground for a seven-word question doesn't it?

Let's start with training. Training sessions that impart vast quantities of information without considerable time for asking questions and practicing are a waste of time. Adults learn when they do, not when they hear. Imagine observing a class on interviewing skills. You watch the students listen to the instructor; some even take notes. A video is shown that presents several situations where interviews go well and go wrong. There is a brief discussion after the video; the instructor asks for questions and answers the few that are asked. People fill out their evaluation forms and leave the room. See any problem with that?

Try another scenario. Imagine observing a class on open-heart surgery. You watch the students listen to the instructor; some even take notes. A video is shown that presents several operations where the surgery goes well and goes wrong. There is a brief discussion after the video; the instructor asks for questions and answers the few that are asked. People fill out their evaluation forms and leave the room. Do you have any desire to have that surgeon operate on you?

You might be questioning whether it's fair to put interviewing skills in the same category with open-heart surgery, but look at it this way. Is the skill set used by a person hiring a key employee for your organization any less important than the skill set of the surgeon who is walking into the operating room where you're the one on the surgical table? Demand that any training program your people are attending has been designed by professionals who know how adults learn and makes practice the most important part of the session.

Once someone has learned a new skill and practiced it in a learning setting, they have to be able to use the skill in a real-life situation. That's the quality-of-work experience part of this question. You wouldn't be comfortable with a surgeon who told you that she'd had extensive classroom experience doing open-heart procedures but that you were going to be her first real patient, would you? You'd want her to have assisted many times and you'd like to know she'd be operating with an experienced surgeon at her side.

How about your mentee? After they've taken that class you agreed upon, how are they going to get the real-world experiences they need to cement their learning in a reality-based context? You need to help them get the right assignments, the right support as they use their new skills, and the right feedback to help them polish their newly learned technique.

And you thought being a coach was a snap.

■ ■ ■

42. Who in our organization do you need to know?

Business, any business, is about people. I will defend that statement at any time, in any place, under any circumstance. Leaders know more people, usually because they've been around longer and had more opportunities to meet and converse with more people inside and outside their organization. When a leader leaves one company to go to another, it is more likely that they can—in the course of their business day—keep in touch with people from their prior organization. Part of the leader's job is to help others make connections. Nowhere is this more helpful than in a coaching and mentoring session. This question is designed to get your mental Rolodex going. You listen to the response to this question and search for a person you can recommend as a connection.

People need to find other people for information, perspective, or advice. Each of these three situations has its own set of requirements.

▌ *Looking for information.* Here you need to help your mentee construct her own questions well so that when she asks for information, she's asking for the right information. Usually you can suggest a phone contact unless the desired information is detailed or lengthy. Make sure you give your mentee permission to use your name as a reference.

▌ *Looking for perspective.* When perspective is the goal of an interaction between two people, a face-to-face meeting is probably required. This is asking for more than a quick answer, and you are sending your mentee to impose on someone's most precious commodity these days—time. In this case, you will probably need to make a phone call of explanation or facilitate the meeting yourself.

■ *Looking for advice.* I once coached a woman who was struggling with issues around balancing her career with her young children. I can remember my own issues of balance well, but my experience was years ago, and things have changed. I called a friend, a successful working mom I know, and asked if she could spend some time with my mentee, helping her figure out some strategies to keep her sanity. Advice is a bigger request than information and perspective, and I needed to put some skin in the game by asking my friend what I could do to repay her. The night I spent having pizza with her kids while she worked late on a critical report was really quite fun.

No matter what form your connection takes, make sure you remind your mentee about the basics of good networking. You learned them from your mother or, if you didn't, borrow my mother's lessons: Please, thank you, and the asker picks up the check.

■ ■ ■

43. What work would you like to be doing in five years?

You don't ask this question so you can hear the answer, you ask it so your mentee can hear their answer. This is a question designed to help people understand that they should dream about their future. Isn't it sad that we need to be encouraged to dream? Ask a six-year-old and they'll give you a list of all the things they want to be and do. Ask a thirty-six-year old, and they'll usually stammer and stutter. Don't let them duck it. "I don't know. Guess I've never thought much about it" can't be an acceptable answer when a leader, acting as a coach, asks this question.

Push. Make them think about it. Make it perfectly clear that there is no right or wrong answer. They aren't committing career suicide if they admit to a secret passion that involves writing the Great American Novel or starting their own business. You won't take them off the promotion list if they reveal that they want your job. Let them know you've got five-year dreams too.

■ ■ ■

▊ QUESTIONS FOR NEWLY PROMOTED LEADERS

44. Why do you think we made you a leader?

Asking a question that requires self-evaluation is valuable for both the asker and the answerer. The answerer gets the immediate challenge of doing the self-evaluation and the reward of the insights they gain.

This question will provide you, the asker, with information on how promotions are viewed within your organization. The reasons individuals ascribe to other people's promotions are often interesting. The reasons they share for their own promotions are even more

> **Every clarification breeds new questions.**
>
> —Arthur Bloch, American merchant

fascinating. You'll get responses that are naive, cynical, and out of left field. You'll get some answers that are insightful, well-thought-out, and accurate. You'll find people who are embarrassed you asked and those who can't wait to talk about it—at length and in great detail. Given this diversity of responses, why ask this question at all? You ask it to determine how well your leadership promotion process is working.

An answer that accurately reflects the balance you strive for between the leadership behaviors your organization desires and the skill set of the person who's been promoted can give you confidence. The right leadership messages are being sent by the process itself as well as the individuals who are being promoted. This is good news for you and your organization. Any time that this match doesn't happen during the answer to this question, you've got some work to do.

Unfortunately, in many organizations, promotions to leadership positions aren't made on identifiable future leadership potential but rather on past technical performance. Don't misunderstand. I'm well aware of the need for high standards when it comes to technical expertise and of the fact that it's often a challenge to find a person who is both technology savvy and people savvy. But, just because it's difficult doesn't mean it's impossible. Just because the technical part of our work is considered the *hard side* and the people part of our work is referred to as the *soft side*, doesn't mean that the hard-side stuff is more important. In fact, one could argue (and many have) that leadership is all about soft-side stuff.

Any omission of the soft-side issues in a new leader's response to this question should raise a red flag that requires your attention. People can't know what they don't know, and a person who's been named a leader may not realize the new scope of their responsibilities. You may need to mentor this person closely as they begin their journey as a leader.

45. What did the best leader you ever had do?

I used to do customer service training until I started viewing poor service as a bonus event that would provide me with more material, a greater sense of job security, and a reason to celebrate. That's a perverse worldview, so I changed the focus of my work.

There was an exercise I did in those workshops that applies here. Since everyone has been a customer, I asked participants to share the worst customer service they'd ever experienced. Then we compiled a list of the characteristics that made those encounters unbearable. I scribbled their answers onto a large flip chart and then told them not to be guilty of any of those behaviors themselves. This technique worked quite well I might add, because we've all been a poorly treated customer and can identify how the transaction went wrong.

The same technique can apply to leadership, especially when you apply it with a positive spin. When you ask, *What did the best leader you ever had do?*, you're asking a new leader to identify the good leadership behavior they've experienced. We've all been led by others and can identify what worked. Listening to their answers and supporting the behavior choices they've made also gives new leaders a sense of confidence about their potential as leaders. Asking new leaders to adopt positive leadership behavior they've experienced and have chosen as beneficial is much more effective than burying them with a laundry list of your own notions of effective leadership.

As your leadership dialogue with new leaders deepens over time, these initial behaviors can be the ones you question them about. As they grow more confident as leaders and as you have more insight into their leadership strengths and development needs, you can suggest other skills that they might want to work on as well as ways to learn and develop them.

46. What do you need to learn to be a great leader?

Why would you ask this question? Why do you ask any question? Questions are asked in order to learn. This question goes to the heart of the philosophy that believes that people aren't born to be great leaders; they're great leaders because they've learned to lead.

(A note of caution for this and the next question. Don't ask these questions if you and your organization don't have the intention or the systems in place to provide learning and support activities for newly promoted leaders. It just isn't fair.)

If I had to guess, I'd predict you're going to hear answers that range from "I don't know" to "Here's my list." Think about your responses to answers that fill that spectrum as I share a few of my ideas.

The person who responds with a list of leadership behaviors they want or need to learn about needs help with prioritizing. If you don't help them focus their leadership learning objectives, they will quickly become overwhelmed by the scope of all they believe they don't know. They need your guidance so they can pick one behavior or skill to work on first. Based on your understanding of the group this person is about to lead and their current leadership skill set, make a few suggestions about places to start as well as what resources are available. Be prepared to follow up with them in fairly short order to make sure they've kept focused and not fallen into the "I'm so overwhelmed I can't do anything" trap.

A response of "I'm not sure yet" requires more questions. You need to help this new leader explore the scope of good leadership skills and find a way to discover where they should start their leadership learning plan. If you've asked, *What did the best leader you ever had do?*, you have some insight into this person's view of good leadership, and you can use that answer as a starting place.

A straight-on "I don't know" response to this question means you've got some work on your hands. My first concern would be to see if this new leader is taking their new role seriously enough. I'd hope that anyone who was stepping into their first leadership position would have spent some time thinking about what they needed to learn in order to become an effective leader. Trying not to let my obvious negative judgment show (that's probably something you wouldn't have to deal with, would you?), I'd indicate that we need to continue this conversation for a while until the right follow-up steps become obvious.

An aside. If you have influence over your organization's training programs, this question should make you curious about how you prepare leaders in your organization. This would be a perfect time to find out.

■ ■ ■

47. How can we support you as you grow into this leadership position?

Please consider this question carefully. Asking it means that you take leadership seriously, and it would be dishonest to ask if you neither have the resources nor the intentions to provide the support you're asking about. But, even if you don't have a formal program for new leaders, you can still support their efforts. You are their leader, after all.

Support in general is a key aspect of a leader's job. In fact, supporting others as they work to get their jobs done is the biggest part of a leader's job. Your supportive actions will take many forms, but they're all just part of a broader support system for new leaders.

Leaders provide support when they act as role models. From the superheroes of our youth to the inspiring figures of adulthood, we've all craved having someone to show us how to behave. This if-I-had-a-pattern-I-could-follow-it stems from our earliest way of learning. As very young children we watched the people around us, imitated their behavior, and learned about how the world worked. Leaders can support by serving as role models.

Leaders provide support when they break barriers for their teams. Leaders aren't leading when they solve problems for their team. But they aren't leading either if they distance themselves from their team's issues. Leaders are right on target when they help a team clarify the problem they're working on, offer a wider perspective on an issue, provide feedback (when requested) on a particular solution, offer access to resources when implementation is imminent, or take a battle farther up in the organization when something falls outside of the team's charter. Leaders provide support when they eliminate appropriate barriers.

▌ ***Leaders provide support when they listen.*** Sometimes people need a sounding board for their thoughts and ideas—not a surface that talks back, but a surface that reflects their own thoughts and ideas so the team can see their work from a fresh perspective. People need a surface that asks questions when clarity is needed. Good listening behavior allows a leader to do all these things. Leaders provide support when they listen.

Practice these, and add other supporting behaviors to your leading repertoire. There is probably no more rewarding work for a leader to do than to nurture new leaders. The bonus is that you'll be a better leader for it.

■　■　■

QUESTIONS DURING A CRISIS

48. Are you all right?

In a crisis this question will mean different things to different people, and that's perfectly okay. Some people will assume that you're asking about their physical well-being and will answer from that perspective. Some will assume you're asking about their mental state and will answer that way. Still others will give you credit for thinking and caring about both. They'll answer with that interpretation in mind. No matter which question they believe you've asked, their answers will be valid.

In times of crisis, people look to their leaders for clues to the behavior that's expected. The last thing a leader should do in emergency situations is to disappear. If you disappear, your people will create reasons for your absence, none of which will be particularly

> Good questions outrank easy answers.
>
> —Paul A. Samuelson,
> American economist

favorable to you or your leadership. Your organization, your leadership team, your people, or, in some situations, the public, can't afford for you to disappear, hide behind spokespeople, stop making eye contact, or utter repeated *No comments*. (There are ways of not making a statement without saying *No comment*. Learn how from a professional.) The bigger the crisis, the more visible, approachable, and accessible leaders need to be. No excuses. No exceptions.

Okay, maybe one little exception. If you're facing a major crisis, one that seriously limits your ability to spend time with each person you need to ask this question of, appoint people to ask and listen in your place. Gather them together and explain that "The first thing we need to do is to check on our team. I want each of you to talk and listen to as many of our people as you can by asking them if they're okay." Then, plan your timetable, send the group out to ask and listen, and regroup to discuss the responses and plan your next actions. This exception does not extend permission to disappear from the eyes of the people who look to you for leadership. I've granted you permission to ease up on the approachability and accessibility, but not the visibility.

If this isn't making sense, let me try one more time. Does thinking about Mayor Giuliani's conduct after September 11th make the picture clearer?

■ ■ ■

49. What do you need to know?

Crisis creates fear, and the only way I know to quell fear is with information. Your job as a leader during a crisis is to be visible, approachable, accessible (see the comments on the previous question), and the fount of all information. Impossible, you say. I guess I agree. It's impossible, and yet a leader needs to figure out how to make it happen during a crisis.

As I see it, the only possibility of pulling this one off is a combination of two things. First, you need to have your own support group that is made up of the smartest people you can find and that can be mobilized quickly. Some need to be people-smart. These are the individuals who know the *soft side* of leadership inside and out. Others need to be technology wizards in whatever technology makes your business run and makes it special. These people won't necessarily be leaders; in fact, some of them will be frontline doers. Just make sure you know who they are and how to get them close to you in a hurry. With your team assembled, you can go to work.

You'll be the point person, talking to people and asking them what they need to know. Some responses you'll be able to answer immediately. Some answers will come from the members of your team. There are some things you're asked for that you or your team won't be able to provide right away. That's where the second part of the strategy comes into play.

Make it the job of those soft-skills experts to keep track of the unanswered questions and the people who asked them. As information becomes available, research is completed, and answers found, it is the job of the soft-skills people to get those details out—delivering the right answers to the right people. If there is a significant time lapse between questions being asked and answers being available, these people will also have the responsibilities for periodic updates and check-ins so no one feels as if the information they've requested isn't important, or even worse, as if they're not important.

If this feels like a lot of work, it is. The scope of your crisis will determine the complexity of your information distribution process and system. Just don't lose sight of what started the need for all this in the first place.

You're the leader. You and your people are living through a crisis. You asked the question a good leader would ask: *What do you need to know?*

50. What do you need?

Now reread the answer to the last question. Probably the team you assembled in response to that question will continue to deal with the results of asking this question. There's one more thing to focus on.

In a time of crisis, when emotions are high, it's tempting, yet disastrous, to promise things you hope you can provide but which, when the question is asked, you aren't sure you can deliver. People don't cut you a lot of slack for these promises. Remember, they hear the promises through their own emotions and often cling to them as literal lifelines. Going back on a promise (even an implied one) with so much emotion invested, is at best uncomfortable and at worst a disaster (potentially bigger than the original crisis).

So what's a leader to do? Only make promises you can personally fulfill by your own authority or out of your wallet. For things beyond those parameters, stop, listen carefully, take notes about the issue or need, and respond with something like the following: "What I've heard is that you need [recap the individual's request]." Pause and wait for confirmation. "What I'm doing with all requests that we can't immediately fill is the same thing I promise to do with yours. I've taken notes along with your contact information. My promise to you is that I will be back in touch with you by [insert a reasonable length of time]. By then we'll have a better grasp of the entire situation and I'll be able to answer your request accurately."

Putting this in your own words and practicing it will make it your own. Discuss it with your crisis team and make sure they understand the impact for all of you when any one of you makes a promise that can't be kept later. Apply the old customer service motto: Underpromise and overdeliver and you'll be all right.

▮ ▮ ▮ ▮ ▮ ▮ ▮ ▮ ▮ ▮ **WHAT DID YOU LEARN?** ▮ ▮ ▮ ▮ ▮ ▮ ▮ ▮ ▮ ▮

If you weren't convinced before, then after reading this chapter you must be sure that most leadership activities include some form of special circumstance. It is these special, unexpected, out-of-the-ordinary moments that define leadership as something beyond simply watching tasks being accomplished, projects being completed on time and under budget, and customers being served. It is what makes art the necessary adjunct to the science of leadership. It's what makes the role of leader an exciting place of creativity.

Leaders in different organizations, different industries, and different teams face different special circumstances. The ones I focused on in this chapter are fairly common. But I don't know yours. Based on your past history in your environment, what special situations do

> **Effective management always means asking the right questions.**
>
> —Robert Heller, American editor

you imagine you'll face in the next twelve months? This would be a great time to use the worksheet on the following pages to make a list of your potential special situations and to brainstorm questions you could use if and when any of those situations actually happened.

I worked with an excellent leader for many years. He often told his team, "Don't bring me any surprises." He meant it, and they learned that he meant it. I watched him talk (to use a polite form of an appropriate verb) to one of his team members when a surprise came through her team and surfaced at the top in his office. It wasn't very pretty and not a really great example of leadership. On the other hand, I had also been present when that surprise unfolded and I watched him handle the customer with the big, long-term problem that he hadn't known about. That conversation seemed to be handled by another man entirely. In fact, if I hadn't been there for both of them, I wouldn't have believed a single person could behave so differently. So I asked.

"Why were you so calm and powerful when you talked to the customer and so out-of-control and unfocused when you talked to your direct report?"

"I've spent years thinking about and creating questions to ask when a customer has a problem," he said. "I just never thought to do the same for a time when one of my team disappointed me."

No matter how long you've been a leader, thinking things through, developing a set of questions that match a situation, and practicing is a really good idea.

▮ ▮ ▮ ▮ ▮ ▮ ▮ ▮ ▮ ▮ **CHAPTER FIVE WORKSHEET** ▮ ▮ ▮ ▮ ▮ ▮ ▮ ▮ ▮ ▮

1. Which of the special situations in this chapter did you find most compelling? Why?

_____

_____

_____

_____

_____

_____

_____

_____

2. What other special situations do you face?

_____

_____

_____

_____

_____

_____

_____

3. What questions do you need to think about for those situations?

_____

_____

_____

_____

_____

_____

_____

4. How will you answer those questions?

_____

_____

_____

_____

_____

_____

5. What is the one thing that you want to remember most from this chapter?

_____

_____

_____

_____

_____

_____

_____

OTHER NOTES

_____

_____

_____

_____

_____

_____

_____

_____

chapter 6

questions leaders
need to answer

WHY IS it that in today's chaotic business environment, many still cling to the belief that having a mediocre answer is better than having a good question? Why is it that after millions of books on leadership have been purchased (and hopefully some have actually been read), people expect leaders to tell rather than ask? I don't know, but I can live with not knowing.

For the last several years I've made it my business to become comfortable being the one who always asks questions. I can't pinpoint what caused me to change my focus from expert answerer to skilled questioner, but I can report on the results. People think I'm smarter, more insightful, and nicer. This chapter is an attempt to help you, a leader, to become a better questioner. The first part of this book has provided the opportunity to learn and practice questions you can use to become known in your organization as a different kind of leader. Now I'd like you to think about answering questions. It occurs to me that after reading this, you might have a question for me. "Chris, just as you convinced me that the role of the leader is about asking good questions, now you're saying that I have to have the answers. I'm confused." I'm tempted to push your buttons and remind you that a moment of great confusion is often the springboard for great creativity and learning, but I won't. I'll answer instead.

There is a difference between leaders who spend their time telling people what to do, think, or feel and leaders who create an environment where followers ask thoughtful questions and the leaders know which ones they should answer. The more questions you ask, the more questions you should expect. This is a good time to add to your skill set.

People will ask you, with varying motives, the question *What do you think?* A moment's thought before answering this question is a good idea. If it is more important for the questioner to state their opinions and understanding, the leader will answer with another question: *More importantly, what do you think?* This technique isn't about evading a question; it's about challenging the questioner to express themselves in an area of their responsibility and expertise. On the other hand, if the *What do you think?* question is a genuine attempt to learn a point of view or tap into a wealth of expertise, the astute leader will answer, adopting the role of educator.

This chapter is designed to help you think through questions that you as a leader may be asked to answer. They're not all the questions you'll be asked. In fact, they're questions seldom asked in most workplaces. These are questions that go beyond the superficial; they ask, in effect, "Who are you and why should I follow you?" They're questions about values and concerns. They have underlying mes-

---

Questions bring us back to human contact.

—Dorothy Leeds,
communications consultant

---

sages; people will have a hard time asking them. Don't kid yourself. Even though people haven't asked them out loud, they've asked these questions silently and determined an answer for you as they watched your behavior. By creating a questioning culture, you'll have the opportunity to actually answer them yourself.

But, even more important, these are significant questions you should be asking yourself. Take the challenge!

■ ■ ■

51. What do you see happening in our organization over the next twelve months?

It's the vision thing. In my favorite leadership book, *The Leadership Challenge* by James M. Kouzes and Barry Z. Posner, the authors remind leaders that it is their job to imagine things for their organizations that are beyond the ordinary. That's why people ask this kind of question. It is their attempt to understand, clarify, and get excited about their future. If they can't get an answer from their leaders, they feel lost, adrift, and frightened.

I've sat in more leadership team meetings than I care to remember during which the leaders asserted how impossible it was for them to answer this question. Their excuses were many. "The things that are happening are confidential." "Once we get things turned around, we'll have time for this philosophy stuff." "The competition is killing us; we may not have a future." "We don't have a clue." These are the responses of leaders who are using their titles under false pretenses. Even with the constraints of confidentiality, can't you say something? How will you turn things around if you don't know what direction you're facing? Why shouldn't we engage our entire team in dialogue to help us understand and beat the competition? How can you not have a clue? Leaders have to talk about the future. All the time. At every opportunity.

What happens during your leadership team meetings? Maybe it's time for you to discuss this question together. Whether you're the team leader or a member, bring it up for conversation. If you lead from the middle of the organization, gather your peers and talk. Too often, everyone assumes that these issues are the responsibility of the organization's *real* leader. Nothing is further from the truth. Real leaders exist at all levels of the organization, and the visions they have need to be part of the ongoing dialogue about the future.

After you have become known as a leader who thinks, talks, and cares about the future, start turning this question back to the people who ask it of you. Help them understand that they help the organization and themselves when they share what they know from their unique perspective.

It will not undermine your credibility as a leader if you talk about your vision for the future based on what you know today and revise your view when circumstances change—as long as you include the changing circumstances along with your revised vision for the future. It will enhance your credibility as a leader if you identify the unshakable values that will guide your own and the organization's behavior, no matter what the future brings. It will focus and uplift your organization if you talk about things beyond the ordinary each time this question is asked.

52. What is the future of our industry?

I've always understood the expression "Can't see the forest for the trees." It wasn't till I moved to northern Wisconsin that I realized not everyone does understand it. It's easy, in this land of wonderful woods, to miss the beautiful expanse as you focus on one scruffy pine—wondering why someone hasn't pruned it. The same thing happens at work.

People get caught in the daily cycle of "Write the to-do list, work on the to-do list," and get frustrated by how many things remain on the to-do list at the end of the day. It would be silly to expect that cycle to be anything but a permanent part of our work life. There will always be more tasks than there is time. There will always be interruptions that usually end up dumping more tasks on our desks. Fast isn't fast enough. Remember when you could blame things on the post office? Overnight delivery services, fax machines, and e-mail technologies have changed forever what we mean when we say, "I'll do it right away." More than ever, we need someone to help us break the cycle of tasks and encourage us to see beyond the day-to-day. Leaders are those people.

Most employees don't have the opportunity to attend trade association meetings or have access to and the time to read industry forecasts, but they need the information obtained by doing both. That's where you come in. As a leader it is your job to understand the bigger picture. How does your organization fit into your industry? How do you rank against your competition? What changes are affecting the way you and your competition will do business in the future? You need to know these things in order to make wise decisions and chart a course into the future. The people at all levels of your organization need to know these things, too. They need to know so they have a better context for understanding management decisions. So they can help customers understand changes in policies and practices. So they can think about their own future. So they have hope.

People get so focused on the task in front of them (the next deadline, the next round of budget cuts) that they seldom lift their heads to look at the big picture. It is in the bigger picture that we can find the hope that will lift us out of daily despair. If you want to call yourself a leader, you should know about the bigger picture, so talk about it.

■ ■ ■

53. What gets you excited about the future?

Have you ever known anyone who's had a brush with death? People's reactions vary, but most often they seem to walk away from the experience vowing to make every minute count. They realize there are no guarantees when it comes to the future, and that's okay as long as they are taking advantage of the present. They greet each piece of the future they're given with joy for the opportunity to experience it. They are excited on purpose. Leaders have a responsibility to show people how to view the future with excitement without having to cope with a near-death experience.

So, what does get you excited about the future? I remember sitting at the dinner table as a child with my brother, mom, and dad. Our family was, in so many ways, a TV family of the '60s. We had dinner together almost every night and talked about all sorts of things. Every time a conversation got mired in a problem, my dad would express his faith that "in the future, technology will fix that."

> I am not a teacher, I am an awakener.
>
> —Robert Frost, American poet

Keep in mind that this was in 1964, before eight-tracks, cassettes, and CDs—before handheld calculators, dumb terminals, and laptops. The princess phone was the latest thing in telephone technology, and if you had a color TV, you were the envy of just about everyone else. It wasn't that my dad was seeing new technology every day. He had just seen enough of the things that were on the drawing boards to marvel at what might happen next. His belief that technology could solve any problem may sound naive, but he was excited about the possibilities. He eagerly read the paper, watched the news, and talked to the people connected with emerging technologies so he could learn. He was energized when he thought about the future.

What does that for you? There are so many people who believe that excitement about the future is a sign of cerebral ineptitude while cynicism marks the intellectual. Oh, please. Cynicism is the mark of a person who spends their time ignoring all the reasons that the universe provides, on a daily basis, for hope and renewal. There are many positions to take between Pollyanna and Dilbert. Leaders need to find their position and talk about what fires them up when they think of tomorrow.

■ ■ ■

54. How do you learn about our customers?

Several years ago, one of the airlines aired a TV commercial that told the story of a leader who gathered his team around a table to announce that one of their oldest clients had just called and fired them. As he handed out plane tickets, he told the team that they were going to visit their customers face-to-face and reconnect with them. "What about you, boss?" asked one of the team members. "Me," he said pulling a ticket out of his back pocket, "I'm going to visit that old client who just fired us." It was a powerful commercial. I think of it often.

Some leaders wouldn't recognize a customer if they bumped into one. Pity. There is a contradiction if you ask the people in your organization about your customers without having any firsthand experiences to add to the conversation. Hearing stories secondhand isn't the same as talking to a real live customer who's frustrated by the failure of one of your products. It isn't the same as seeing how your services enable another entire organization's processes. It doesn't match the relationships developed with customers over time.

There are leaders, of course, who do work to create opportunities to interact with their customers. Unfortunately, those relationships are often limited to the largest customers or those customers who have complained loudly enough or demanded emphatically enough to get an audience with a leader. These contacts, desirable as they are, do not provide a clear enough picture. What's a leader to do? Here's an idea—and a challenge.

Pull out your organization chart and identify twelve areas where you haven't had, or don't have, much occasion to interact with customers, and make it your plan to spend time with a person in one of those areas each month for the next twelve months. Spend the day with an installer. Listen in with a customer services representative. Make some sales calls, clean bathrooms with a janitor, and review financials with an accountant. Listen to their customer interactions. See your policies and procedures in action. Ask questions to determine how many of your experiences that day are typical. Experience for yourself the needs and concerns of your customers. Get smart.

The next time you sit in a leadership team meeting, think of all you'll have to say!

P.S. Don't forget to send thank-you notes.

■ ■ ■

55. How do you know what I do in my job?

I'm often hired to do skill-building workshops for frontline employees. The particular skill doesn't seem to matter; the same question is asked by participants, "Are you doing this program for our managers/leaders?" Usually the answer is no, but I've come to believe that their question isn't grounded in a concern about the skill set of the leadership team. It's grounded in the concern of many people that their leaders are clueless about what they do on a daily basis. They believe that the people who make decisions that affect their daily lives have no idea what their daily lives are all about.

Let's face it. Leaders have access to (almost) unlimited support possibilities. They control budgets and assignments. They get the latest technology, the best bathrooms, and preferred parking. Now, don't get defensive—these statements might not apply to you, but I bet there are people in your organization who believe they're true. Perception becomes reality, remember? In all fairness, it's important to say that most people in your organization don't have the foggiest notion of what you do every day either.

What's a leader to do? Here's an idea—and a challenge. (Some of it may seem familiar from the last question, but read carefully. There are some subtle differences.)

Look at your organization chart and identify twelve areas where you haven't had, or don't have, much occasion to interact with employees, and make it your plan to spend time with a person in each of those areas each month for the next twelve months. Spend the day with an installer. Listen in with a customer services representative. Make some sales calls, clean bathrooms with a janitor, and review financials with an accountant. Listen to their customer interactions. See your policies and procedures in action and the effect they have on workflow, the quality of work life, and productivity. Experience one of their days. Ask questions to determine how many of your experiences that day are typical. Experience for yourself the needs and concerns of your employees. Get smart about them.

Don't stop there. Pick another area each month, and invite someone in your organization to spend the day with you. Ask them to shadow you through meetings, phone calls, and lunch. Encourage them to ask questions and answer them honestly. Help them get smart about leadership.

■ ■ ■

56. How can I advance in our organization?

Have you ever listened to the radio station WIIFM? I'm surprised if you haven't. It has the power to broadcast all over the world, and my experience, both personal and professional, leads me to believe that everyone tunes in to this station—sooner rather than later. WIIFM stands for What's In It For Me. Get it?

Face it, we all run ideas, decisions, and problems through the filter that answers the question *How will this affect me?* When we can estimate the effect, even if it's not positive, we can move into action. When we can't figure out what's going on, we often find ourselves paralyzed by the fear of the unknown. This question is an attempt to understand an important workplace process.

Promotions within an organization are often quite mysterious. It appears that some people rise quickly based on *who* they know with little regard to *what* they know. Some talented, smart people appear to be overlooked, and sometimes a good guy wins the promotional lottery. It's hard to figure out if promotions are based on skills, personality, or hat size. Jobs are posted and filled on the same day. No wonder people are confused. You need to help clear up the confusion by talking about the answer to this question.

First of all, do your homework. How are people chosen for promotion? Does your organization use their values as a primary screening tool for advancement, or does job-specific competency supersede all other considerations? Are your policies administered uniformly, or are they bent on a regular basis? Does *who you know* matter more than *what you know?* Once you have a clear picture of your current reality and implement any changes that you may decide are necessary, start composing your response to this question.

I believe that there are three parts to a promotion decision. Your answer should cover all three.

1. *What skills does this person bring to the job?* Every position needs technical competencies in both the hard- and soft-skill areas. People must understand that they need to take charge of their own skill development if they want promotional opportunities within the organization. You need to help them discover what skill sets the organization expects for a successful future.

2. *What behaviors does this person exhibit in their current position?* Jobs are not just about getting the task done; they're about *how* you go about getting the job done, too. People need to understand that their ability to work effectively on a team, offer creative ideas, and learn continuously will affect their promotional opportunities within the organization. You need to help them match their behaviors with the organization's values.

3. *What attitudes does this person bring to work every day?* Organizational attitudes are the composite of the attitudes of all people who work there. People need to understand that most often, attitudes are an initial screening device for promotion. You need to ensure that all employees are given feedback regularly, not just once a year at review time, about how their attitudes are perceived throughout the organization.

57. How do you make decisions?

After a fifteen-year on-again, off-again quest, I found a copy of a book I remember from my early childhood, *I Decided*. Rereading it after more years than I care to share with you, the story was just as I remembered. A little girl goes shopping with her mother and is allowed to pick one toy. She weighs her options, thinks through the possibilities, and makes an informed decision. She can't wait for her father to come home from work so she can tell him about her choice. I loved that book and made my mother read it over and over until I could read it for myself. It described my decision-making process to a *T*. Have you ever thought about how you make decisions? Before you can answer this question and explain your decision-making process to someone else, it might be helpful to spend some time reviewing exactly how you do make decisions.

The employees who ask you (or who would ask you if they thought they could), *How do you make decisions?* are trying to understand what goes on behind the scenes so they can better understand the decisions you make. They will learn to make better independent decisions if you help them envision the kinds of things you consider as you make decisions. You could share what kinds of decisions are hard for you and which ones are easy. You could share with them how you gather data as well as how much data you gather before you feel confident of the facts behind an issue. You could let them know under what circumstances you go with your gut feeling and when you need logic to prevail. You could share how you decide who you go to in order to bounce ideas and possible solutions around.

You could, if you're really brave, talk about bad decisions you've made and how you came to make them. Even better, you could talk about how you learned from a bad decision and how you changed your decision-making behavior because of it. You could ask the person questioning you how they make decisions and what they've learned about decision-making in their previous jobs. You could assure them that organizations are stronger when different people employ many different ways of making decisions as long as everyone does their homework before they decide. You could challenge them to become better decision-makers.

I could lend you my copy of *I Decided*.

58. How do you take time to think?

This question can be tricky if your answer is *I don't* or *I've heard of people who try something like this.* How do you find time to think? Not to solve problems or put out fires, but just to think about things both big and small. I know, I know: you're so busy every day there's never any time for quiet reflection. Maybe on your next vacation? This is the worst form of self-deception leaders can engage in. If the leader isn't stepping away from the day-to-day activities in their part of the business to think, who is? Ignoring the need for thinking allows seemingly healthy, active businesses to fail because of the change they never saw coming…until it was too late. Please don't fall into that trap—it's awfully hard to get yourself out. Here are six suggestions to help you find time to think. After you've practiced them for a while, you can use them, with assurance in your voice, to answer this question.

1. *Make an appointment with yourself.* This is the least you can do, so before another week goes by, do it! Schedule a thirty-minute, hold-my-calls, can't-be-changed meeting with yourself and keep it. During these thirty minutes, think. Don't write, read magazines, or clean your desk. Think. It would be great if you could do it with your office door open. Don't let people interrupt. Tell them you're thinking and you'll get back to them shortly.

2. *Take a walk.* A short fifteen- to twenty-minute walk at an almost brisk pace will provide a great thinking environment. Since this is a short burst of thinking, why not try it with a question in mind? Not a day-to-day problem, although this works well for that, too, but a general *I need*

to think about that some day issue. Here are some possible topics that fit this technique.

- What's changing in our environment that we haven't thought about?

- What new skills will our team need in the next year?

- What barriers exist to our team's success this quarter?

3. *Do your daily exercise routine without distractions.* Distractions are a room full of people talking, your favorite morning or evening news show, or the video of last night's episode of *The West Wing*. As you work out, let your mind wander and follow where it goes. Thinking is an amazing process that requires relinquishing control and enjoying the journey to insight. Distractionless exercise is a great opportunity to experience it.

4. *Listen to Mozart.* As I write this, the *Mozart at Midnight* CD is playing in the background. Read the book *The Mozart Effect* by Don Campbell for all the research, but take it from me—Mozart helps you think. You can turn flying time into thinking time if you carry earphones and Mozart with you.

5. *Engage in a hobby that you enjoy and that requires repetitive movement with your hands.* Here are a few I can think of that work: Woodworking. Knitting. Gardening. Painting. Playing an instrument. Golf could work if you did it alone. Hiking, again if you're alone and if you swing your arms as you go. Ironing. (Please don't spread this one around.) Any of those strike your fancy? It's the repetitive

nature of the hand movements that seems to trigger creative thinking. If you don't currently do any of these or anything else that fits the criteria, try one. Don't worry—when you find the right thing for you, you'll know immediately.

6. *Take a field trip.* Go to a museum, an art gallery, or a library. Visit a mall, sit in a competitor's parking lot, or fly a kite. Do it by yourself or take a colleague. At the end of your excursion ask yourself, *What did I see or experience today that taught me something about my work or my life?* Don't push for the answer, but don't give up too quickly. There's always something there; you just need to think till you find it.

All of these ideas require two things: the courage to try them and tell others what you're doing, and paper and pencil to jot down the great thoughts that will surface. Be careful—this thinking stuff can become contagious. I guarantee it.

■ ■ ■

59. What makes you angry in the workplace?

My friend Kathryn Jeffers wrote a book called *Don't Kill the Messenger: How to Avoid the Dangers of Workplace Conflict*. In the Introduction, she paraphrases Aristotle's words on anger. He believed that anyone can become angry, but to be angry with the right person, to the right degree, for the right purpose, and in the right way, is not easy. If you know how to be angry with the right person, to the right degree, for the right purpose, and in the right way, and if you have asked three people who care enough about you to tell the truth for verification of your skill set, skip the rest of this question. If not, read on.

Anger in the workplace is a tricky thing. It is most often misused, misdirected, and misunderstood. Most of us are not comfortable dealing with raw emotions. We get uncomfortable with glad, sad, and mad and go to great lengths to avoid them. We haven't been educated to react appropriately when we're either the giver or the receiver of these emotions. Learning to understand, control, and utilize conflict in a positive way takes commitment, practice, and hard work.

Unfortunately, leaders often think they are exempt from the commitment, practice, and hard work it takes to make anger a tool rather than an outburst. In many organizations, the stories about a leader's rage are legendary, and they're usually not stories with happy endings. It is highly unlikely that you or any other members on your leadership team will succeed by using anger as a management tool. If you or one of your colleagues uses anger or rage as a technique, this would be a great time to stop it.

This does not mean that you shouldn't think about or talk about what makes you angry. Even though you may pride yourself on containing your anger (trust me on this), people around you know when you're angry. Knowing what makes you angry is helpful for both you and the people around you.

Several years ago I realized that having to go over information or instructions people had already agreed upon made the hair on the back of my neck stand up. All of my ability to help a learner learn, and my ability to keep calm and display infinite patience, disappeared. When people ask me to go over old agreements, my jaw clenches, my breathing gets shallow, and I start talking in short, clipped sentences. I don't yell, rant, or rave. The effect, however, is the same. People know I'm angry, and I know they don't know why. This is my problem, as anger so often is, and I've learned that letting people know what's happening to me—and that it isn't their fault—is helpful for both of us. So, answer this question. It will be good for you and for others!

■   ■   ■

60. How do you measure success?

Recently, four of us gathered around a table to play cards. Of the four, one knew all the rules, two knew some of the rules, and the fourth thought she'd played the game once in her life. We played a practice hand to give everyone the opportunity to get a feel for the rules, and then we began playing the game for real. Several rounds into the game, our expert played a winning card. We looked at her with blank stares, and she said, "Oh, I guess I forget to tell you about this move." You can imagine our indignation and the discussion that followed about her winning hand. We've all felt that way at one time or another. We wanted to win, we were playing by the rules, and then someone told us that we really didn't know the whole story. Success wasn't an illusion; it was just a little different from what we were led to believe. (Just in case you're wondering, she won the hand but didn't win the game.)

Success can be a very elusive commodity, especially when you don't know what success is. One would think that if an organization has a set of values, it would be pretty easy to figure out what the rules of success are. If your values say the customer is number one, you'll want to consider the customer's needs and wants in everything you do. If respect for people is high on your organization's values list, you'll want to work on relationships as you get your job done. And if your organization lives their stated values, you'll be right. But not all organizations do what they say.

Leaders have three choices when they want to answer this question. They can review the organization's values with the questioner and help clarify the specific behaviors that match the stated values. They can apologize that they haven't done their job as a leader and get to work on a set of values that are meaningful for their situation.

Or they can change either their existing values or their behavior if the two don't currently match. No matter which of these three options fits your situation, you've got to get the message out to everyone: "This is how we play the game." No fair slipping in a rule or two later.

▌ ▌ ▌

61. What are you learning?

In a recent interview on the *Today* show, the musician Jon Bon Jovi told Matt Lauer how much he enjoyed working as an actor with Matthew McConaughey on the movie *U-571*. As an inexperienced actor, Bon Jovi looked to McConaughey as a leader and wasn't disappointed. Bon Jovi said that it wasn't what McConaughey said but what he did that helped him. Leaders teach by example whether they know they're doing it or not. Do you remember the first time an adult said to you, "Do as I say, not as I do"? Did it strike you as ridiculous at the time? If it didn't then, it certainly should now. Your development as a leader won't go very far if you don't learn this lesson. People inside and outside of your organization will learn more from you about leadership, for good or ill, from what you do than from what you say.

Learning about learning is a hot topic in many workplaces. Businesses in general have reached the conclusion that if they're not learning about their customers, themselves, and their future on a daily basis they're losing the race. I've observed many management team meetings where leaders have discussed learning strategies and opportunities for their people to get smarter. I haven't listened in on conversations where they've challenged each other and reported on their personal learning goals. And that's a problem. People will believe that learning is part of their job in your organization by watching whether or not you're learning.

So, let's talk about what you're learning. I hope you can answer this question with two things in mind. First is that you'd be excited to share the skill you're learning that will make you better at doing your job. It would be great if you could also share how you're learning. Is it a formal process or a self-study situation? You would tell how you were taking what you've learned and practiced and applied it in a real-life situation. You would be willing to share how you might have failed as you tried new skills and how you appreciated the feedback you got from others as you practiced. You would look and sound excited as you described how this learning was making your work easier, more efficient, and more fun.

Then, you would move on to telling us about what you were learning in your personal life. Your face would light up as you described your movement into uncharted waters. Who your teacher was. How often you got to practice what you were learning. How you realized that this personal learning was giving you insights about your business situation—an unexpected bonus. How something could be frustrating and fun at the same time.

After a conversation like this, I'd know you were a lifelong learner and I'd be challenged. Way to go, leader!

■ ■ ■

62. How do you stay positive?

I'd like you to try a little experiment. Remember the first day of your first real job. What happened that caused you to hide the expression on your face so no one else could see the silly grin that spread from ear to ear? Remember what triggered the response and what the response felt like.

Cynicism is a disease that is pervasive in our society and, like a cancer, it holds the possibility of our death. Listen to people in your workplace talking about a new hire. "Did you see the new kid in accounting? Grinning from ear to ear, filled with new ways to fix all our problems." "Yeah, what a hoot! Don't worry, just give him a month, and this place will wipe that grin off his face."

Variations of that conversation get repeated over coffee in organizations from coast to coast and I've never heard of one incident of a leader who has walked over and said, "Excuse me, but don't ever let me hear something like that again! In our organization we want people to join us all fired-up about the possibilities and to stay that way for their entire career. And, by the way, if you don't feel excitement about what you do here on a daily basis, maybe your résumé needs dusting off!" Can you see yourself delivering that message? I hope so.

In order to deliver that message convincingly, you need to be enthusiastic about your job and show it. Not necessarily in big ways, but in small, consistent ways. Body language, tone of voice, expressions of glee, and expressions of concern are all ways people make judgments about how you're feeling about your job. Leaders who are excited about what they're doing on a daily basis create environments where cynicism has a hard time taking root.

As a leader, you are not, however, expected to be *up* all the time; you do get to be human. Discouraged, tired, and frustrated happen to all of us. You do need to have strategies to make your own attitude adjustments and, upon occasion, do them publicly. A lot to ask of a leader, isn't it? Just remember, it's why they pay you the big bucks.

63. How do you re-ignite your enthusiasm for your job?

Everyone gets down in the dumps. The trick is not to stay there. Especially when you're the leader. So, how do you re-ignite your enthusiasm? I call my grandson Quinn. At the time I'm writing this he's twenty-one months old, and his favorite word is WOW! (The caps and the exclamation mark are deliberate—you can hear them both in his voice.) When I call, no matter what day, what time, my son Paul says, "Quinn, do you want to talk to Grandma?" I can hear him running to the phone saying "WOW!" I really wouldn't need the conversation (and truth be told, at twenty-one months it isn't much of a conversation) to go on. My spirit is lifted from whatever pushed it down by a simple word delivered with enthusiasm, "WOW!"

What about you? Do you take a walk around the plant? Substitute a session at the gym for lunch? Meditate? Pray? Call your mother or your favorite uncle? See, it doesn't matter what you do. It does matter that you have something that you know will work, that you do right away. Something you can do without thinking, and that works about 98 percent of the time. Something that doesn't take much time, expense, or equipment. Because you're the leader. Your team needs you to be enthusiastic. It's a big part of your job.

Please don't relegate this to some of that silly "Life is just a bowl of cherries" nonsense foisted on a gullible population by overpaid motivational speakers. This is about hope, an overlooked attribute that should be a leader's stock-in-trade. Leaders owe their people hope at the same time they're providing the truth about tough situations. It's their job to be role models for re-igniting enthusiasm when times are difficult.

So you need a plan. What fires you up? A day off to re-group? A vacation to re-create yourself? A conversation with your favorite customer? A talk with your newest employee? An e-mail to your mentor? A phone call to Quinn? I'll be glad to share the number.

■ ■ ■

64. What do you love about your job?

Did the word "love" in this question make you raise an eyebrow, cough nervously, or think about moving on to the next page? These questions are going to get increasingly personal as the pages turn, and you're going to have to make a decision about whether or not you're going to stay with them. Being a leader requires that you go to a deeper level instead of staying on the surface. Oh, you can manage by skimming the top of issues, emotions, and people, but you can't lead from there.

Leadership requires thinking about and acting on things that occur beneath the surface. It requires that you care enough to confront. People who have heard me talk about teams have heard me say, "Hate is not the opposite of love. Apathy is." Leaders can't be apathetic. So we need to talk about love, enthusiasm, fun, and meaning. Can you handle that?

What do you love about your job? I hope it doesn't take too long for you to answer. It's easy for leaders to get so caught up in all the important things they're supposed to do that they forget the things that brought them to their profession in the first place. I remember when my Aunt Elsie, who became a nurse during World War II, realized that she wasn't happy being a nurse because nurses no longer spent much time with patients. Her first impulse was to quit nursing since the part of the job she loved the most no longer occupied most of her time, but she came to understand that, by changing the kind of nursing she was doing, she could do more of what she loved. She left the hospital setting and became a visiting nurse. She devoted the rest of her nursing career to direct patient care.

So let me ask the question again. *What is the part of your job that you love?* The part you would do if they paid you or not?

What are the ways you can work more of those activities into your schedule?

Just one other thought. What about loving the things you have to do? There is a great greeting card that says, "In order to love what you do, don't do what you love, love what you do." Pretend I've just sent you that card. Hold it in your hands, stare at it for a while, and ponder the message. Just some more food for thought.

■ ■ ■

65. What do you do just for fun?

I was doing a team-building session for a group of system-types in a large organization. We had claimed our space in the corporate conference center and made it ours for the two days of our session. By the afternoon of the first day, it was a mess. Flipcharts covered the walls, candy wrappers littered the floor, and colored makers were everywhere. Subgroups were taking the challenge of designing and producing a race-winning paper airplane seriously. The groups had decided to put some distance between each other to avoid industrial espionage and left the room to work outside in the warm spring sunshine. I was alone in the meeting room.

The door opened and a three-piece-suit type stuck his head in the room, looked the space over and said, with a touch of disapproval, "What's going on in here?"

"A session on team building," I calmly replied.

"Oh," he said as he backed out of the room, "You're not doing real work then."

I no longer react to such ignorance; I just feel pity. All those people who haven't figured out that learning can be fun, work can be fun, and fun can be work, just don't get it. Organizations thrive when people have fun as they work together. Leaders are the ones that make having fun at work a legitimate behavior.

Fun. Ah, you remember fun, don't you? *What do you do just for fun?* Think about the last time you grinned from ear to ear, giggled, or laughed out loud. That was a hint, you were having fun. Hopefully it's not taking you too long to think of an example. The more confusing, demanding, and complicated our lives become, the more we need fun as a counterbalance. On really stressful days in our office, we've been known to go outside to make snow angels, have a Koosh ball battle, or dissolve into fits of tear-producing laughter over really stupid jokes. What happens during stressful times in your office?

How do you feel about fun? Is it an integral part of your work and personal life? Do you believe it has a place in your off-duty life, but not in the workplace? Is fun a word that's lost its place in your vocabulary? Think about it. You never know when someone might ask!

■ ■ ■

66. What gives your life meaning?

This is the BIG question, and only you can answer it. But answer it you must. Leaders owe it to themselves as well as the people they lead to go deeper into their own motivations, their hopes, and their dreams. Business schools don't require a course in "Understanding Your Personal Mission" for graduation, nor do many family conversations involve parents sharing their purpose in life with their children. Most of us grow up believing that scores get kept based on things like home runs hit, beauty contests won, and amounts on annual W-2 forms. What a pity.

Think of a person who had a great positive influence on your life. How did that happen? Was it the size of their office that so impressed you that you decided right then and there that you were going to strive to be a great leader? Was it the tale of an exotic vacation, a fancy car, or a prestigious title that convinced you to follow someone's footsteps? I rather doubt it. More likely it was a quiet word spoken at the right moment, an encouraging smile after you spoke up at a meeting, or a short note of congratulations for a job well done that caused you to say, "This is a person I want to emulate."

My friend Mary Marcdante said, "When you're on purpose, life fits." How does your life fit these days? If tomorrow were your last day on this planet, would your list of regrets be longer than your list of accomplishments? People who are clear about the meanings of their lives find it much easier to make decisions about the big things, to prioritize the activities that fill up their days, and to know, really know, what's important. There is great peace of mind in knowing how to answer if someone asks, *What gives your life meaning?*

In his wonderful book *The Eagle's Secret*, David McNally quotes Maureen Gustafsen, CEO of the Mankato Chamber and Convention

Bureau as saying, "We all have a significant role to play. It is our duty to determine that role and our obligation to fulfill it." I couldn't agree more. That's why this question appears twice in this book. It's a question you need to both ask and answer. Organizations that are filled with people who both unapologetically ask and thoughtfully answer this question are places with a very bright future.

■ ■ ■

■ ■ ■ ■ ■ ■ ■ ■ ■ **WHAT DID YOU LEARN?** ■ ■ ■ ■ ■ ■ ■ ■ ■

Early on, I advanced the theory that great leaders don't have all the answers, but they have great questions; and now, as promised in the beginning of this chapter, I've put you in the position of having to provide answers. How did it feel?

Could you tell that these are not your usual let's-go-ask-the-boss kind of questions? I hope so. Managers understand that they need to be factual, organizational, and functional resources for the people on their teams. Leaders know that their questions and answers must go beyond that—into areas of philosophy, ethics, and feelings.

> **All the answers we ever get are responses to questions.**
>
> —Neil Postman, Chair, Department
> of Culture and Communications,
> New York University

Leaders are skillful at asking the right questions, at the right time, of the right people. Leaders are equally skilled at giving the right answers, to the right question, in the right context. They think about the questions that need to be asked, learn from the answers, and take action appropriately.

They know when to ask, when to answer, and when to listen. They really mean it when they say, "Don't worry, there's no such thing as a stupid question." They have the courage to respond with an "I don't know" when they don't know. They're comfortable answering a question with silence.

In *Confessions of an Accidental Businessman*, James Autry wrote, "This has to do with the transition from manager to leader being fundamentally a leap from the external to the internal, from the life outside to the inner life, from a preoccupation with doing to the acceptance of being as the defining characteristic of leadership." I couldn't agree more!

■ ■ ■ ■ ■ ■ ■ ■ ■ ■ **CHAPTER SIX WORKSHEET** ■ ■ ■ ■ ■ ■ ■ ■ ■ ■

1. Which of the questions in this chapter did you find the most challenging? Why?

_____

_____

_____

_____

_____

_____

_____

_____

2. What behaviors do you want to change based on what you've learned in this chapter?

_____

_____

_____

_____

_____

_____

_____

3. What other questions might you need to answer?

_____

_____

_____

_____

_____

_____

_____

_____

4. How would you answer those questions?

_____

_____

_____

_____

_____

_____

_____

_____

5. What is the one thing you want to remember most from this chapter?

_____

_____

_____

_____

_____

_____

_____

OTHER NOTES

_____

_____

_____

_____

_____

_____

_____

answers for
special situations

LET'S TAKE a look at special situations from a different perspective. How about those times when you're asked a question and it's your answer that's a problem? In this chapter we'll look at a few of these situations.

The more you practice asking questions, welcoming questions, and answering the questions that are asked of you, the easier all this questioning business becomes. But there's always the question that throws you off your game, the question you don't know how to answer, or the question you just don't want to answer. What happens then? Reading this chapter will give you some ideas, though not all the ideas—just enough to help you to your own solutions.

During an interview on the *Today* show, Sir Ian McKellen was asked about the lessons he learned from doing years of Shakespeare. He replied simply, "Never underestimate the script." That's a good lesson for leaders, too. Thinking about how you'd deal with the sit-

> **Questions are never indiscreet. Answers sometimes are.**
>
> —Oscar Wilde, Irish writer

uations described in this chapter and how scripting an answer could work for you (even if your script doesn't quite reach the level of Shakespeare) will boost your confidence as a leader who can answer just about any question.

■ ■ ■

DURING A BUSINESS CRISIS

67. What's happening?

The response to this question is less about completeness than it is about frequency. In the midst of a crisis, leaders can have an unimaginable list of people competing for their time and attention. It appears that the people on their teams often go to the bottom of the list. I think this is a mistake. Your people will be patient and understanding because you have, of course, been straight with them before this situation arose, but they need something to be patient and understanding about.

Don't fall into the trap of thinking you should wait until you've gotten everything figured out or have a complete picture before talking to your team. Frequent communication in settings where they can physically see you is best. Even when there is nothing new to say, visibility always works in your favor.

Take a deep breath before you talk. Calm yourself. Make good eye contact. Let your feelings show appropriately. Finish by promising an update and KEEP YOUR PROMISE.

■ ■ ■

68. What's going to happen next?

If you ignore the advice from the last question, you probably won't have to face this question. Not what I'd recommend, however. When people ask *What is coming next?*, it is good news. This question means they can see a little beyond the immediate, and it is usually an indication that you've been doing a good job of answering the *What's happening?* question.

At any given time during a crisis, you may or may not have an answer to this question. That's okay. Just continue to tell what you know and what you can tell when you can tell it. Make the time of your next update common public knowledge and keep it, even if you have nothing new to add. Be visible. When you see some future possibilities that you can share, do so. Label them as speculation or good bets or whatever term actually describes their probability. If they become more probable, announce that. If they fade as possibilities, announce that.

Three things a leader can do wrong during a crisis are to disappear, to start and then stop communications, and to make promises in the heat of the moment that they can't keep later. Practice not doing these three things when there isn't a crisis, and you'll do okay when there is.

■ ■ ■

69. What's going to happen to me?

This is a question that is asked but not vocalized, so you may have to bring it up yourself. In any crisis people look closest to home first. That's nothing to be ashamed of—it comes from the survival instinct in all of us. But sometimes, when we realized we've stopped thinking about the big picture and have focused on our own situation, we feel guilty.

As a leader you need to remember that people are thinking about the effect on their own lives even though that might not be what they're saying. You might have to say it for them. You might have to bring up a question you know you can't answer. How's that for walking out on a limb voluntarily?

The same issues we explored for the last two answers apply here. Just because you don't know the complete answer doesn't mean you can give an answer and promise more information as it becomes available. Remember to keep your promises, however, or none of the good will you had before the crisis will last.

■ ■ ■

70. Am I going to have a job next month?

Questions during a crisis are less about facts and more about emotions. This question comes straight from the gut, not the head. Most leaders I've watched acted as if it were just the opposite. When they ignore the emotions and speak only to the facts, they lose their team or their audience. That's why *Yes* is such a tempting answer for a leader and why leaders are tempted to use it when it doesn't apply. Nowhere is that more obvious than when it comes to job security. As much as you'd like to be able to answer this question with a *yes*, don't do it unless you are 100 percent certain.

Of course, not much in today's world is 100 percent certain, so your answer to this question is apt to be closer to *I don't know*, and there are some comments about that answer in the next chapter. But you're in front of your team right now and don't have time to page through a book to find a formula for success. (Don't bother looking for one. In this kind of situation, formulas don't exist.) Think of it this way. What would you want to hear in this situation? A forthright *I don't know* or a lot of fancy words and phrases used to obscure the fact that what is being delivered is no answer at all?

Maybe there is a formula after all. Don't ignore the emotions you're dealing with. Tell the truth, sincerely and frequently. Update as promised in clear and simple language. Don't make promises you can't keep. Keep the promises you do make, and stay visible. Don't shy away from the emotions; learn to deal with them. You'll be a better leader for it.

■ ■ ■

71. What's the long-term impact of this crisis?

By the time this question is asked, the immediate crisis has probably faded. This question becomes the basis for dialogue about the future. As a leader, you want to avoid the position of just being a dispenser of wisdom most of the time. During a crisis it is appropriate for you to be an answerer; now that the crisis has passed, it is time for you to encourage your team members to search for their own answers.

Answering a question with a question can be seen as evasive—and it often is. But when this technique is used judiciously, it can be quite effective in bringing groups together to think. Review the following dialogue to see this technique in action.

> "What's the long term impact for us, boss?"
>
> "Actually I'm thankful that we've got enough breathing space to ask about long-term anything. From what you've seen and heard, what do you think?"
>
> "I haven't heard much, everybody's keeping a pretty low profile, but I did see some new orders being processed. That's got to be a good sign, doesn't it?"
>
> "I think so, too. Why don't we get the team together and share what everyone's been hearing, and then I'll let you know what I've been told. Maybe together we can start to build a picture of the future."

▌ DURING A MERGER OR ACQUISITION

72-73. What's going to change? What's going to happen to my job?

Some questions that come up during mergers and acquisitions are pretty easy to answer if you're willing to face people who won't be happy with the answer. The answer to these questions falls into that category. This won't be a one-time conversation; what you're about to read is a very abbreviated version of a real conversation, but it should give you some insights into the role you're going to play.

"What's going to change?" or "What's going to happen to my job?"

"Why don't you count on everything changing."

"You're kidding, right? It's all not going to change. It couldn't possibly do that."

"I know we'd all like to believe that not much will change, but my experience is that in situations like ours, change becomes the norm."

"I hate change."

"You're not the only one. I like to keep in mind that while change is often hard, it can also be exciting. When I look back, some of the toughest changes in my life turned out to be times of growth and new opportunities."

"Yeah, but it's still hard."

"Yeah, it's hard. Let's keep talking. We'll be going through it together."

Leading people during times of change demands that a leader get smart about how change affects people. Like other questions in this book, these questions are all about emotions, not facts and figures. If you try to answer them with facts and figures, you'll miss the real point of the question. Helping people sort through their emotions is tough and probably wasn't covered in your job training.

If you're not developing your expertise around how people react to change, this would be a perfect time to start. Change sneaks up on you when you least expect it.

74. Who will be my leader?

This is a flattering question depending on the nonverbal behaviors that go with its delivery. As a successful leader, you're allowed to bask in the warm feeling that this question conjures up for a few seconds before you proceed to answer it. Time's up.

In *Creating You & Co.*, William Bridges suggests that " Job security no longer resides in a job (*any* job). It resides in your ability to add value to what some organization does...." Try reading it with a few words changed. Job security no longer resides in a boss (*any* boss). It resides in your ability to lead yourself in a way that adds value to what some organization does. Great leaders work with the members of their teams to help them develop their own leadership skills.

Like good consultants and good parents, these leaders aim to work themselves out of a job. They know that if they lead with this attitude, their team will always value their leadership just as the consultant will have clients that want them back and the parents will have adult children who will always value their opinion. Leaders of the old school—command-and-control types—are shortchanging the people they lead and, ironically, themselves. They'll never experience the joy of watching someone they've coached succeed on their own. They'll never get to marvel at the moment when the student outpaces the teacher, and they'll be poorer for it.

If you've never thought about this before, use this question as a wake-up call. You need to review how you're preparing your people to lead themselves or transition to another leader. You need to help your team own their values, their work, and their success.

If you've done your homework, *Who's going to be my leader?* will be an easy question to answer. *Nothing's going to change; you'll keep leading yourself.*

75. Will our values last?

My guess is that you won't be able to answer this question, but you ought to be very glad someone asked it. Leaders help establish, shape, and nurture organizational values. A leader who goes home at night knowing their team lived their values that day has done the job of a leader well. But values are fragile things. When they are ignored or talked about but not practiced, they revert to words on a page rather than guides to make decisions by.

People in organizations that have gone through mergers or acquisitions will recount stories that reveal that integrating systems is much easier than combining cultures. Mismatched values, opposite views of the future, or competing styles of leadership can be insurmountable obstacles to success.

So, what's a leader to say when asked this question? How does a leader nurture hope when it seems in short supply? By being authentic. Authentic means saying, "I don't know." Authentic means sharing your feelings and saying, "I worry about that, too." Authentic means being brave during change: "This is hard for all of us." Authentic means hanging in there: "I promise I'll be here with you tomorrow." Authentic means keeping your team focused: "During this time of change, let's build our reputation as a team by focusing on our customers." Authentic means being a leader.

■ ■ ■

▌ **DURING THE PERSONAL CRISIS OF AN EMPLOYEE**

76-78. What will the organization do to support me? What are my benefits? What will this mean for my career?

Up to this point, we've explored questions leaders need to ask and answer. We haven't looked at any questions leaders should not answer. Now is the time, and these three questions are perfect examples of questions leaders shouldn't answer by themselves.

Visualize a briefing after a plane crash. The chief investigator from the National Transportation Safety Board (NTSB) is behind the microphone giving an overview of the work the investigators have done so far. A reporter asks a technical question about a report of wind shear experienced by other pilots in the same airspace the day of the crash. The chief investigator listens intently and says, "Let me call John up to answer. John is our wind shear expert and I know he's been looking into that." The leader steps aside and John takes over. When that question is answered, the leader returns to the lectern and takes the next question. At several points during the briefing, the leader defers to others on his team who have the specialized knowledge to answer the question asked.

As you visualized this event, did you ever have a problem with the leader's credibility? I doubt that you did or would. Smart leaders know what they know and, even more importantly, they know what they don't know. When faced with questions outside their expertise, they don't make things up, they don't promise things that might make sense on the surface but have serious consequences they can't envision, and they don't brush off the question. They bring forward people with specialized expertise, or they know how to connect the questioner with the expert in a hurry.

Most of your situations won't involve press conferences and reporters clamoring for answers. Questions like the ones that can arise during an employee's personal crisis occur during one-on-one time where the temptation to answer a question in order to help someone in a time of need will be strong. You must resist the temptation. People in crisis will cling to any answers and promises, and if you've given one that your organization either can't or won't fulfill, you're in trouble.

These are questions that need to be answered by your human resources professionals, sometimes by your legal council, or by people within your organization who have the appropriate expertise. If you have an EAP (Employee Assistance Program) program, they can help. The key to answering employees' questions when they're in the midst of a personal crisis is to know your limitations, know the kind of support your employees can find elsewhere in your organization, and take the responsibility for finding the professional who can help effectively.

■ ■ ■

WHAT DID YOU LEARN?

It is important that you give careful answers to the questions asked of you in these special situations. When you're on the receiving end of the questions, there are a few behaviors to practice and remember. Look for opportunities to role-play your answers and find ways to get feedback as you work on and develop your answering skills.

1. *Engage your brain before you open your mouth.* Most people are uncomfortable with silence, so they rush to fill it. Resist. Give yourself permission to think first and answer second.

2. *If the answer is I don't know, say I don't know.* Don't ever make things up because your ego thinks leaders are supposed to have the answer to everything. (There is more about an *I don't know* answer in Chapter 8.)

> The uncreative mind can spot wrong answers, but it takes a creative mind to spot wrong questions.
>
> —Sir Antony Jay, British writer

3. *Make sure you understand the question before you answer it.* Repeating a question or asking for clarification is a good idea. While the question is being clarified, you also get a few more minutes to frame your answer.

4. *When you've finished your answer, make sure you check with the questioner and find out if you've actually answered their question.* If you get a *yes*, you can move on. If you get a *no* or a questioning look, you need to continue the dialogue.

▌ ▌ ▌ ▌ ▌ ▌ ▌ ▌ ▌ ▌ CHAPTER SEVEN WORKSHEET ▌ ▌ ▌ ▌ ▌ ▌ ▌ ▌ ▌ ▌

1. What special situations in Chapter 7 did you find most compelling? Why?

_____

_____

_____

_____

_____

_____

2. What other special situations do you face?

_____

_____

_____

_____

_____

3. What questions do you need to answer in those situations?

_____

_____

_____

_____

_____

_____

4. How will you answer those questions?

_____

_____

_____

_____

_____

_____

_____

5. What one thing do you most want to remember from this chapter?

_____

_____

_____

_____

_____

_____

_____

OTHER NOTES

_____

_____

_____

_____

_____

_____

chapter 8

delivering
tough answers

HERE WE are almost at the end, and in a way we're back where we started. What's your model for a leader? If it's still the fount of all wisdom, the worshiped guru, or the benev-

> Sometimes, the question is more
> important than the answer.
>
> —Plato, Greek philosopher

olent know-it-all, answering the questions in this chapter will be tough. If, on the other hand, you've developed a model of the leader as a seeker of truth, a coacher of individuals, or a teacher who learns, they'll be simpler.

These answers aren't fun to give. They deal with situations where you have to say no, keep information secret, or tell people things they don't want to hear. These answers are the right answers to give in difficult situations—they're tough, and you're the leader who has to deliver them.

■ ■ ■

Answering when the answer is *I don't know*

We established early on that becoming a leader does not ensure that you become the fount of all wisdom. That being true, you're bound to face a question where you simply don't know the answer. Don't panic.

First, think through the question again to determine if you've been asked a fact question or an opinion question. If you've been asked an opinion question, you have to answer. You're the leader; you're expected to have opinions. If you've actually never thought through this particular issue, you can say, "Good question. I've never been asked that before. Let me think for a moment and come back to this one." Then your obligation is to return to the topic and express your opinion.

If you've been asked a fact question, and you don't know the answer, don't (under any circumstances) make up an answer. Your credibility as a leader as well as your reputation in your area of expertise will plummet faster than you can imagine when you're found out (and you will be). In this situation, simply reply, "I don't know, but I'll check the facts and get back to you." Now your obligation is to do what you promised. Check the facts and get back to the person who asked the question. Your reputation will be enhanced as long as you follow through.

Answering when the answer is *No*

No means *no*, but leaders and parents often fall into the same trap and use it to mean *maybe*. This is a place when your past track record will serve or haunt you. If you consistently say *no* when you mean *no* and say *maybe* when you mean *maybe*, then, over time, answering with a *no* will be easier.

However, if you consistently deliver *no* responses without providing a context for the *no*, you will be seen as an autocratic leader. Never having aspired to that particular title, I've always chosen to focus on the context that produced the *no* answer.

One of a leader's most significant roles is that of teacher; delivering context is the best place I know to see leader-as-teacher in action. Saying *no* tells people what not to do, but it doesn't teach them anything. When leaders take the time to describe the process they use to reach a decision, they are teaching. If you explain the data you reviewed, the conversations you had and with whom, and the decision-making criteria you used, others will not only understand this decision, but they'll be able to follow your process the next time it's their turn to make a decision.

Who knew how valuable a *no* could be?

■ ■ ■

Answering when there isn't an answer

Some questions just can't be answered. Not because you can't reveal information or because all the facts aren't in, but because there just isn't an answer.

Life is full of questions that can't be answered. How big is the universe? How high is up? Why do bad things happen to good people? These questions exist, and people aren't happy about them. I believe that most people think of questions as if they were mystery novels. Some are so easy that you know who did it right from the beginning of the book. Others are more complex and take a while to figure out. Good mystery novels, like good questions, challenge you to think, and when you do, there's great satisfaction. Then there's the complex mystery you've read with great attention. You've struggled with red herrings and thought you had it solved several times only to realize you were wrong. You approach the end of the book defeated but happy that the ending will explain it all. You turn to the final chapter and realize that someone has torn the last two pages out of the book. There is no answer to the mystery.

Some questions can never be answered just as some mysteries will never be solved. People don't like that fact, leaders don't like it, and I don't like it. But it is the truth. So when you're faced with a question that can't be answered, do the only thing possible—tell the truth.

Answering when you can't answer

State secrets, confidential information, competitive analysis—you know the whole thing, and someone asks you a question about it. The butterflies start immediately. The person who asked is trustworthy, and you've been their leader for a long time. They know you know. You know that they know that you know. You can't answer. You've been cautioned, warned even. Your hands are tied. Isn't being a leader fun?

Try this answer on for size. "Sometimes it's difficult to be a leader. One of the most difficult parts of leadership for me is when my responsibility to the members of my team comes into conflict with my responsibilities as a leader in our organization. This is one of those times. I will not be able to be as open with you now as I have in the past. That being said, I want you to know that I will tell you all that I can as soon as I can. I realize this puts a strain on our relationship as a team. I can only hope that my behavior in the past will allow you to trust my behavior now."

I know, it's not perfect, but it's the best I've ever been able to come up with. If you've found a better answer, please share it with me.

■ ■ ■

Answering when no one wants to hear the answer

You know the truth; they know the truth. It's just that no one wants to hear it. Flash back to your college days and hear the groan that followed the professor's "quiz tomorrow" announcement. Remember your reaction when your child's teacher called and said that your firstborn wasn't working up to their potential. These both represent important messages delivered to people who are hoping against hope not to hear them. There are lots of these moments in business. Leaders who have messages to deliver that no one wants to hear. Layoffs. Mergers. Reorganizations. Projects that get cancelled. Mandatory overtime. In these situations the message is fixed. No amount of wordsmithing is going to make hearing about a 10 percent reduction in your workforce sound or feel better. Focus on the delivery.

DON'T send this message via voice mail, e-mail or Webcast. It will be tempting, and I know you can build a case for both efficiency and cost savings, but getting a message out isn't the same as having a message heard.

DO deliver the message in person (or deputize others to stand in for you at various locations) so you can see your people and they can see you. The only way you can come close to guarantee that an I-don't-want-to-hear-it message is received is to look into people's eyes.

Be creative and be thoughtful. Denial isn't a river in Egypt. If you underestimate the criticality of delivering a consistently understood message and verifying its reception, you're going to have a very long day.

Answering a question that's just too personal

This one's pretty short and sweet. Just because you're a leader and someone has asked you a question doesn't mean you always have to answer it. It is perfectly okay to establish some boundaries, usually around your personal life, that you're not willing to cross. As long

> **Don't answer a question just because it's asked.**
>
> —Marilyn Mobley,
> American PR specialist

as you afford others the same respect with regard to their own boundaries and you let the people around you know about your limits, you should be okay. All you need to say is, "That question falls in an area that you already know I don't discuss."

■ ■ ■

■ ■ ■ ■ ■ ■ ■ ■ ■ ■ **WHAT DID YOU LEARN?** ■ ■ ■ ■ ■ ■ ■ ■ ■ ■

Tough or simple? Probably a little of both. Leadership is many things, and on some days it's hard. Delivering answers that fall into the categories in this chapter isn't fun. Most leaders, especially the kind that would be reading this book, like to be open, approachable, and fun. Answering with "No, I can't tell you," or "You're not going to like to hear this" doesn't qualify as open, approachable, or fun. But there are times when they're the right answer to give.

Recently I was part of a task force dealing with some sensitive issues. At the end of our long, into-the-wee-hours-of-the-morning meeting, we all agreed that the information and substance of our conversation needed to be held in confidence until all the parties involved could be notified. It was my job to deliver the messages the

---

Bromidic though it may sound, some questions don't have answers, which is a terribly difficult lesson to learn.

—Katharine Graham, American newspaper publisher

---

next morning. Imagine my dismay when I started to deliver those messages and discovered that some of the individuals had already heard, via the grapevine, the outcome of our deliberations.

My disappointment was not so much that the information was leaked. That just made me mad. My disappointment stemmed from the fact that my colleagues, people I considered leaders, didn't know how to answer a question that required a tough answer.

I'm sorry, we've agreed to keep the meetings confidential.

No, I can't answer that.

You can ask me that several times, and my answer will still be the same.

I will give you that information as soon as it's possible.

Leaders need to deliver a tough answer once in a while. I guess it just takes practice.

▌ ▌ ▌ ▌ ▌ ▌ ▌ ▌ ▌ ▌ **CHAPTER EIGHT WORKSHEET** ▌ ▌ ▌ ▌ ▌ ▌ ▌ ▌ ▌ ▌

1. Which of the tough-answer situations in this chapter did you find most compelling? Why?

_____

_____

_____

_____

_____

_____

_____

2. What other types of answers would you find it difficult to deliver?

_____

_____

_____

_____

_____

_____

_____

3. How would you deal with communicating those answers?

_____

_____

_____

_____

_____

_____

_____

4. What is the one thing you want to remember most from this chapter?

_____

_____

_____

_____

_____

_____

_____

OTHER NOTES

_____

_____

_____

_____

_____

_____

_____

_____

_____

_____

some final questions

"The important thing is not to stop questioning. Curiosity has its reason for existence."

—Albert Einstein, American scientist

"We can only learn and grow if we are willing to ask a lot of good questions."

—Dr. Alan Gregerman,
American business consultant

"How can we improve this?"

—Walt Disney, American entrepreneur

Here we are at the end. So:

What will you take away from this journey we've made together? Have you started your own list of questions?

> I hope so. Go back and look at the worksheets. Maybe you'll find inspiration in the Appendix. Start a list on your handheld organizer or buy a new notebook. Good questions show up at the most unusual times.

Do you find yourself with a broader view of leadership?

> This question demands a short stop. At the beginning of this book I said that I believed that you'd rather be a good leader than a poor one and that being a great leader would be even better. Having a bigger view of what leadership is and can be is worth the investment you put into reading this book.

Are you one who takes big steps or baby steps?

> Try some baby steps first. Pick your favorite question and work with it for a while. Gauge people's reactions and monitor your comfort, as you become a leader who asks questions.

Have you given yourself goals and a deadline?

> Oh, for heaven's sake. You've been around too long not to know why this is important.

Do you need to ponder more?

> Important. Give yourself time to think things through

and get comfortable with new actions. Just don't use pondering as an excuse for not starting.

Are you feeling confident or anxious?

Either is okay. Both at the same time are understandable.

What support system can you count on?

Who can you enlist to support your personal change effort?

Is leadership worth being passionate about?

Yes. One might even say that a leader without passion is no leader at all.

Do these questions never end?

The questions never end, or you should hope they never end because questions are linked with learning, and learning is linked with growth, and the only alternative to growth is death. Not a good choice.

Are we done now?

I am. You're just starting.

Little children ask questions all the time because they're curious. Adults are often afraid to ask questions because they are afraid of appearing stupid, ignorant, or uninformed.

I admire leaders who ask questions like children. I know they're brave.

> *What would I do if I knew I could not fail?*
> *If I believed would the wind always fill up my sail?*
> *How far would I go, what could I achieve*
> *Trusting the hero in me?*
> *What would I do today if I were brave?*

From *If I Were Brave*
Words and music by
Jana Stanfield and Jimmy Scott

appendix

Good Questions from Other Leaders

As a part of the research for this book, I conducted an e-mail survey asking leaders around the world to share their favorite questions. Their response was overwhelming. People took time out of their busy days to think and write about their experiences with questions. The following list is a representative sample of their responses for your review. I've included them so you could find and use some of them for yourself and to inspire you to start your own list.

My thanks to all who participated and my heartfelt gratitude for a community of leaders who are as passionate as I am about the importance of questions for a leader.

What's the risk of doing nothing?
—Jeff Blackman, CSP consultant and speaker

Does what you are doing make you and the organization grow?
—David C. Palmer, U.S. Army

What ideas do you have?
—Phyllis McConnell, Dell Computer Corporation

What if none of this works? What next?
—Shirley Garrett, professional speaker and author

How do we WOW this customer?
—Ivy Mathieu, Cox Communications

What difference will you make for the organization today?
—Vivian Londos, The Human Resource Store

How do you face disappointment with grace?
—Nora Butcher, speaker and author

How will we know when it is enough?
—Claudia Brogan, University of North Carolina

How can you ensure that this plan will be effective?
—Ann Hutchinson, Bureau of Land Management

How can we make a change for the better of the business?
—Jerry Dowen, Oshkosh Truck Corporation

If you owned the company, would you do it the way you are proposing?
—Joe Tripalin, CUNA Mutual Group

What do you think?

> —Judy VonTress-Pretto, Hernando and Valencia
> Properties, Inc.

Do you honestly have the time to put this new task on your calendar?

> —Steve Sorenson, CUNA Mutual Group

What should I do to make sure you've got no worries on this project?

> —Marc Vermeulen, Eurosem

What support do you need from me to make that happen?

> —Lynette Dornink, Lands' End, Inc.

Do you think the culture of an organization can be changed by one individual? Why or why not?

> —Linea M. Cicinelli, WCI Communications

How are you doing today?

> —Dennis C. Dakin, Potts Welding and Boiler Repair

What is it that we want to accomplish in the long run?

> —Shirley Garrett, professional speaker and author

I know it can be done…but should it be done?

> —Rose Kilsdonk, Shaker Advertising Agency

What's the new learning here?

> —Else Tamayo, University of San Francisco

Suppose you owned the situation, what steps would you take?

> —Kathy Trammell, Harborstone Credit Union

How did you get into this profession?
> —Dave Jennings, CAE, SPHR, American Society for Training and Development

Why have we always done it this way?
> —Marcia Britton, Pechiney Plastic Packaging

How can I be part of the solution, not part of the problem?
> —Diane Marema, Museum of Science and Industry

What can I do to make myself more valuable to the company?
> —Carol Rouzpay, The Regence Group

Can you give me specific feedback on how I can be a better leader for our organization?
> —Susan C. Stevens, Alliance Data Systems

If you could make one decision that would put this organization on a more positive course, what would it be?
> —Lyn Huntley, IRS

What is your true passion?
> —Suzy Rettig, Countrywide Home Loans

What are the greatest needs and challenges facing your customers?
> —Pam Gartmann, Delta Dental Plan of Wisconsin

What are you taking time to do these days?
> —Paula Briki, IBM

Is there a better way to do this?
> —Lillian Roberts, Pitt County Memorial Hospital

How can I make a difference to the team?
—Michael T. Reimer, Safety Solutions Incorporated

What have you done today to develop your leadership skills?
—Neil J. Anderson, TESOL

Does this meet the highest standards of quality?
—John Dermody, City of Phoenix

Do we all have the same sense of purpose and understanding
of the desired outcomes?
—Cheryl K. Duvall, Mercer University

What about your job inspires you to help a customer?
—Candy Prince, Bank of America

What went wrong?
—Maura Schreier-Fleming, Best@Selling

What questions should we be asking our customers?
—Michael A. Podolinsky, Team Seminars

Why?
—The question most commonly identified as a great question

Use these questions to start your list. If you'd like to add some
questions to our list, please e-mail them along with your comments
to Chris when you visit www.LeadersAsk.com. I'm looking forward
to the dialogue.

Suggested Reading

Autry, James A.: *Confessions of an Accidental Businessman: It Takes a Lifetime to Find Wisdom* (Berrett-Koehler, 1996).

Autry, James A. and Stephen Mitchell *Real Power: Business Lessons from the Tao Te Ching* (Riverhead Books, 1998).

Bell, Chip R. and Heather Shea: *Dance Lessons: Six Steps to Great Partnerships in Business & Life* (Berrett-Koehler, 1998).

Bennis, Warren G.: *Learning to Lead: A Workbook on Becoming a Leader* (Perseus Press, 1997).

Blank, Warren: *The 9 Natural Laws of Leadership* (AMACOM, 1995).

Block, Peter: *The Answer to How is Yes: Acting on What Matters* (Berrett-Koehler, 2002).

Bridges, William: *Creating You & Co.: Learning to Think Like the CEO of Your Own Career* (Addison Wesley, 1997).

Buckingham, Marcus and Donald O. Clifton: *Now, Discover Your Strengths.* (Free Press, 2001).

Campbell, Don: *The Mozart Effect: Tapping the Power of Music to Heal the Body, Strengthen the Mind, and Unlock the Creative Spirit* (Quill, 2001).

Corbin, Carolyn: *Great Leaders See the Future First: Taking Your Organization to the Top in Five Revolutionary Steps* (Dearborn, 2000).

Eales-White, Rupert: *Ask the Right Question! How to Get What You Want Every Time and in Any Situation* (McGraw-Hill, 1998).

Farson, Richard: *Management of the Absurd: Paradoxes in Leadership* (Simon and Schuster, 1996).

Finlayson, Andrew: *Questions that Work: How to Ask Questions That Will Help You Succeed in Any Business Situation* (AMACOM, 2001).

Gelb, Michael J.: *How to Think Like Leonardo da Vinci: Seven Steps to Genius Every Day* (Dell Trade, 1998).

Gelb, Michael J.: *Thinking for a Change: Discovering the Power to Create, Communicate, and Lead* (Harmony Books, 1995).

Goleman, Daniel: *Emotional Intelligence* (Bantam, 1997).

Goleman, Daniel: *Working with Emotional Intelligence* (Bantam, 1998).

Gregerman, Alan: *Lessons from the Sandbox: Using the 13 Gifts of Childhood to Rediscover the Keys to Business Success* (Contemporary Books, 2000).

Helgesen, Salley: *The Web of Inclusion: A New Architecture for Building Great Organizations* (Currency Doubleday, 1995).

Hesselbein, Frances, Marshall Goldsmith, and Richard Beckhard, eds.: *The Leader of the Future: New Visions, Strategies, and Practices for the Next Era* (Jossey-Bass, 1996).

Jeffers, Kathryn: *Don't Kill the Messenger: How to Avoid the Dangers of Workplace Conflict* (Link Publications, 1996).

Kawasaki, Guy with Michele Moreno: *Rules for Revolutionaries: The Capitalist Manifesto for Creating and Marketing New Products and Services* (HarperBusiness, 1999).

Kouzes, James M. and Barry Z. Posner *The Leadership Challenge* (Jossey-Bass, 1996).

Leeds, Dorothy: *The 7 Powers of Questions* (Perigee, 2000).

Leeds, Dorothy: *Smart Questions: The Essential Strategy for Successful Managers* (Berkely, 1987).

Maurer, Rick: *Beyond the Wall of Resistance: Unconventional Strategies That Build Support for Change* (Bard Press, 1996).

McCoy, Thomas J.: *Creating an "Open Book" Organization…Where Employees Think & Act Like Business Partners* (AMACOM, 1996).

McNally, David: *The Eagle's Secret: Success Strategies for Thriving at Work and in Life* (Dell Publishing Co., 1994).

Paulson, Terry: *They Shoot Managers Don't They? Managing Yourself and Leading Others in a Changing World.* (Ten Speed Press, 1991).

Peters, Tom: *The Circle of Innovation: You Can't Shrink Your Way to Greatness* (Knopf, 1997).

Senge, Peter, Art Kleiner, Charlotte Roberts, Richard Ross, and Bryan Smith: *The Fifth Discipline Fieldbook: Strategies and Tools for Building a Learning Organization* (Currency Doubleday, 1994).

Sinetar, Marsha: *The Mentor's Spirit: Life Lessons on Leadership and the Art of Encouragement* (St. Martin's Press, 1998).

Stone, Florence M.: *Coaching, Counseling & Mentoring: How to Choose & Use the Right Technique to Boost Employee Performance* (AMACOM, 1999).

Wheatley, Margaret J.: *Turning to One Another: Simple Conversations to Restore Hope to the Future* (Berrett-Koehler, 2002).

index

National Transportation Safety
Board (NTSB), 186
network
helping employees to, 115
situations that require a,
115-116
NTSB, *see* National
Transportation Safety Board

Open-Book Management
elements of, 48
as a type of organization,
48-49
optimism
as key to happiness, 17
in the workplace, 161-162
organization
changing the collective
behavior of an, 75
one-word description of an,
104
values in an, 75-76

partnership, with customers, 37
Pauses, using when questioning, 2
personal questions, responding to,
198
Peters, Tom, xiv
policy, customer dissatisfaction
with, 33
postponing action, 21
pre-work questions, xiv
Prichard, Bob, 88
Posner, Barry Z. 138

procedure, customer dissatisfaction with, 33-34
promises, making, 129
promotions, how people are
chosen for, 148-149

questioning
oneself, importance of, 9
questions
attributes of good, 67-68
customer service recovery, 28
follow-up, 4
for new employees, 106-107
for oneself, 9-26
inexperienced, 2
leaders should answer, 135-172
supplemental, 207-211
that don't have answers, 195
that shouldn't be answered,
186, 196

rewarding
clients, 40
customers, 39-40, 57
employees with benefits, 77-78

Shea, Heather, 38
silence, as effective questioning
tool, 2, 102-103
skills
improving employee's,
113-114
real-life application of, 114
"soft side" of work, 119